ANATHEMAS
and
ADMIRATIONS

BY E. M. CIORAN

Anathemas and Admirations
Drawn and Quartered
History and Utopia
On the Heights of Despair
A Short History of Decay
Tears and Saints
The Temptation to Exist
The Trouble with Being Born

ANATHEMAS
and
ADMIRATIONS

✳

BY

E. M. CIORAN

Translated from the French by
RICHARD HOWARD

Foreword by

EUGENE THACKER

Arcade Publishing • New York

Contents

	Foreword	vii
1	On the Verge of Existence	3
2	Joseph de Maistre	22
3	Fractures	79
4	Valéry Facing His Idols	90
5	The Lure of Disillusion	110
6	Beckett	129
7	Meeting the Moments	137
8	Saint-John Perse	152
9	Exasperations	160
10	Mircea Eliade	179
11	That Fatal Perspicacity	189
12	Caillois	205
13	Michaux	211
14	Benjamin Fondane	218
15	Borges	223
16	Maria Zambrano	227
17	Weininger	229
18	Fitzgerald	232
19	Guido Ceronetti	242
20	She Was Not of Their World	246
21	Foreshortened Confession	248
22	Rereading . . .	251

Foreword

by Eugene Thacker

We like to imagine that poets die poetic deaths. One thinks of Shelley, who, after having reportedly seen his doppelgänger, drowned off the coast of Tuscany while sailing out to sea in his boat, the *Don Juan*. Or Nietzsche, the "mad" philosopher and iconoclast who suddenly collapses in Turin while witnessing the flogging of a horse, his tear-leaden arms thrown around the animal's neck. In the 1990s, an emaciated, elderly man with sharp eyes and wavy hair is found sitting on the side of the street somewhere in Paris's Latin Quarter. He is lost. He can recall neither the way back home nor even his address. He is taken home. Eventually he stops eating. After an accidental fall, he is brought to a hospital. He drifts in and out of lucidity, rarely recognizing those closest to him. He stops speaking entirely. After slipping into a coma, Emil Cioran dies, on June 20, 1995.

For Cioran, the twilight philosopher who once noted "the stillborn are the most free," the end came not with melodramatic flair but gradually and quietly, though it was no less tragic. For several years, the Romanian-born writer had been grappling with Alzheimer's. Writing became more and more difficult. Traveling, lectures, and interviews were impractical. Even a walk out the door took on an almost absurd risk. But Cioran's final silence was, in a way, a long time coming. By the early 1980s, he was finding it more and more difficult to write, though the themes of his writing—pessimism, despair, melancholy, and a certain ecstatic antagonism towards the world—these continued to find their way into his increasingly sparse work. Now well into his seventies, he and Simone Boué continued to live in their Rue de l'Odéon apartment, where he divided his time between long walks in the Jardin du Luxembourg (where he and Samuel Beckett would often cross paths) and writing aphorisms in the cheap, multicolored Joseph Gibert notebooks he had been using for years, and that piled up on his desk in the hazy light of his top-floor writing alcove.

The present volume is a hybrid of Cioran's last two major publications. In 1986, the solitary stroller who once wrote: "Solitude: so fulfilling that the merest rendezvous is a crucifixion," published a book about friends and colleagues entitled *Exercices d'admiration*. It collected short articles written between the 1950s and the 1980s; some of them are about writers with whom Cioran had long-standing friendships (Samuel Beckett, Mircea Eliade, Henri Michaux), while others were about writers with whom he shared a certain temperament (Jorge Luis Borges, F. Scott Fitzgerald, Paul Valéry). There are lesser-known names, too: the Spanish philosopher María Zambrano, the Italian journalist Guido Ceronetti, and the Romanian-Jewish poet Benjamin Fondane.

The list is highly eclectic and situational, and between each essay, Cioran's tone varies widely. Sometimes his writing becomes a hymn that sings the praise of an author, sometimes it takes on a personal, even autobiographical form, and sometimes the writing is cagey and contentious—often Cioran's tone will encompass all of these at once. Of Beckett, for instance, Cioran has this to say: "He lives not in time but parallel to it, which is why it has never occurred to me to ask him what he thinks of events." Of Borges, he writes: "The misfortune of being recognized has befallen him. He deserved better. He deserved to remain in obscurity, in the Imperceptible, to remain as ineffable and unpopular as nuance itself."

Exercices d'admiration is accompanied here by another, quite different book. Struggling with the gradual loss of his memory, in 1987 Cioran publishes *Aveux et anathèmes* (which could be translated as "Confessions and Curses"), a short book of aphorisms on the persistence of time, memory, and mortality. Composed of short, staccato fragments, the writing has all the urgency of a last word, and yet the almost tranquil distance of a documentarian: "How age simplifies everything! At the library I ask for four books. Two are set in type that is too small; I discard them without even considering their contents. The third, too ... serious, seems unreadable to me. I carry off the fourth without conviction." Following the publication of *Aveux et anathèmes*, Cioran decides to stop writing altogether. But it is a gesture already in his mind early on. In a 1980 letter to a friend he notes: "Even the idea of writing makes me queasy, and with it comes disgust, failure, and a complete lack of satisfaction that, not daring to admit this to itself, turns sour."

True to form, Cioran's final writings were the result of a lived contradiction. A hermit singing the praises of others, an amnesiac obsessed with the persistence of memory and time. Circumstance or chance has deprived Cioran of the romantic death; all that remains is writing that leads to its own silence. But if there is a "poetic" image of the later Cioran, perhaps this is it.

＊

In any book governed by the Fragment, truths and whims keep company throughout. How to sift them, to decide which is conviction, which caprice? One proposition, a momentary impulse, precedes or follows another, a life's companion raised to the dignity of an obsession. . . . It is the reader who must assign the roles, since in more than one instance, the author himself hesitates to take sides. The epigrams constitute a sequence of perplexities — in them we shall find interrogations but no answers. Moreover, what answer could there be? Had there been one, we should know it, to the great detriment of the enthusiast of stupor.

ANATHEMAS
and
ADMIRATIONS

1

On the Verge of Existence

✳

W HEN CHRIST HARROWED HELL, the Just
under the old law — Abel, Enoch, Noah — mistrusted his
teaching and made no answer to his call. They took him
for an emissary of the Tempter whose schemes they feared.
Only Cain and those of his race adhered to such doctrine,
or professed to, and followed him out of hell. Such was
the doctrine of Marcion. "The wicked prosper," that old
objection to the notion of a merciful or at least honorable
Creator — who consolidated it better than this here-
siarch? Who else so acutely perceived its invincibility?

✳

Amateur paleontologist, I have spent several months
pondering the skeleton. Result: no more than a few
pages. . . . The subject, it is true, scarcely warrants prolixity.

✳

Applying the same treatment to a poet and a thinker
strikes me as a lapse in taste. There are realms from which
philosophers ought to abstain. To dissect a poem as if it
were a system is a crime, even a sacrilege. Oddly enough,

the poets exult when they do not understand the pro-
nouncements made upon them. The jargon flatters them,
gives them the illusion of preferment. Such weakness de-
means them to the level of their glossators.

*

To Buddhism (indeed, to the Orient in general), Nothingness does not have the rather grim signification we attribute to it. It is identified with a limit-experience of light
or, if you like, with a state of luminous absence, an ever-
lasting radiant void: Being that has triumphed over all its
properties, or rather non-Being supremely positive in that
it dispenses bliss without substance, without substratum,
without support in any world at all.

*

Solitude: so fulfilling that the merest rendezvous is a
crucifixion.

*

Hindu philosophy pursues deliverance; Greek — with
the exception of Pyrrho, Epicurus, and a few unclassifiable
figures — is a disappointment: it seeks only . . . truth.

*

Nirvana has been compared to a mirror that no longer
reflects any object. To a mirror, then, forever pure, forever
unemployed.

*

Christ having named Satan "Prince of this world,"
Saint Paul, to go one better, struck home: "God of this
world." When such authorities designate our ruler by
name, who is entitled to *disinherited* status?

*

Man is free, save for his depths. On the surface, he does
as he likes; down there, *will* is a meaningless syllable.

*

To disarm the envious, we should take to the streets on crutches. Only the spectacle of our collapse can humanize, to some extent, our friends and our enemies.

*

Rightly, in every age it is assumed we are witnessing the disappearance of the last traces of the earthly paradise.

*

Christ again: according to one Gnostic source, he ascended — in abhorrence of *fatum* — to trouble celestial arrangements and to prevent any questioning of the heavenly bodies. In such confusion, what can have happened to my poor star?

*

Kant waited until the last days of his old age to perceive the dark side of existence and to indicate "the failure of any rational theodicy." . . . Others have been luckier: to them this occurred even before they began to philosophize.

*

Apparently matter, jealous of life, seeks to discover its weak points and to punish its initiatives, its betrayals. For life is life only by infidelity to matter.

*

I am distinct from all my sensations. I fail to understand how. I even fail to understand *whose* they are. Moreover, who is this *I* initiating the three propositions?

*

I have just read a biography. The notion that all the figures it describes no longer exist except in this book strikes me as so intolerable that I have had to lie down to avoid a collapse.

*

What entitles you to fling my truths in my face? You

are taking a liberty I deny. Granted, all you allege is correct, but I have not authorized you to be frank with me. (After each outburst of rage, shame accompanied by the invariable swagger — "At least there's some life in that" — followed in its turn by even greater shame.)

*

"I am a coward, I cannot endure the pain of being happy." To sound someone out, to *know* him, it is enough to see how he reacts to Keats's avowal. If he fails to understand immediately, no use continuing.

*

Affrightment: a pity the word should have vanished with the great churchmen.

*

Man being an ailing animal, any of his remarks, his gestures, has *symptomatic* value.

*

"I am amazed that so remarkable a man could have died," I once wrote to a philosopher's widow. I realized the stupidity of my letter only after mailing it: to send another would be to risk a second blunder. With regard to condolences, whatever is not a cliché borders on impropriety or aberration.

*

In her seventies, Lady Montague admitted she had ceased looking at herself in a mirror eleven years before. Eccentricity? Perhaps, but only to those ignorant of the calvary of daily encounters with one's own . . . countenance.

*

What can I speak of save what I feel? And right now I feel nothing. Everything seems erased — suspended. Let me not be proud of this, nor embittered by it. "In the course of the many lives we have lived," says *The Treasure of the True Law,* "how often have we been born in vain, how often have we died!"

*

The further man advances, the less he will have to convert to.

*

The best way to get rid of an enemy is to speak well of him everywhere. What you say will be repeated to him, and he will no longer have the strength to harm you: you have broken his mainspring. . . . He will still campaign against you, but without vigor or consistency, for unconsciously he will have ceased to hate you. He is conquered, though unaware of his defeat.

*

Claudel's famous edict: "I am for every Jupiter, against every Prometheus." We may have lost our illusions about revolt, yet such an enormity wakens the terrorist slumbering in us all.

*

One holds no grudges against those one has insulted; quite the contrary, one is disposed to grant them every imaginable virtue. Alas, such generosity is never to be met with in the injured party.

*

I haven't much use for anyone who can spare Original Sin. Myself, I resort to it on every occasion, and without it I don't see how I should avoid uninterrupted consternation.

*

Kandinsky maintains that *yellow* is the color of life. . . . Now we know why this hue so hurts the eyes.

*

When we must make a crucial decision, it is extremely dangerous to consult anyone else, since no one, with the exception of a few misguided souls, sincerely wishes us well.

*

To invent new words, according to Madame de Staël, is the "surest symptom of intellectual sterility." The remark seems truer today than it was at the beginning of the last century. As early as 1649, Vaugelas decreed, "No one may create new words, not even the sovereign." Let writers, and especially philosophers, ponder this ban even before they start thinking!

*

We learn more in one white night than in a year of sleep. Practically speaking, the adoption of tobacco is much more instructive than any number of regular naps.

*

The earaches Swift suffered from are partly responsible for his misanthropy. If I am so interested in others' infirmities, it is because I want to find immediate points in common with them. I sometimes feel I have shared all the agonies of those I admire.

*

This morning, after hearing an astronomer mention "billions of suns," I renounced my morning ablutions: what is the use of washing one more time?

*

Boredom is indeed a form of anxiety, but an anxiety purged of fear. When we are bored we dread nothing except boredom itself.

*

Anyone who has passed through an ordeal patronizes those who have not had to undergo it. . . . The intolerable fatuity of patients who have survived an operation. . . .

*

At the Paris-Moscow exhibition, my amazement in front of the portrait of the young Remizov by Ilya Repin. When I knew him, Remizov was eighty-six years old; he lived in a virtually empty apartment his concierge wanted for her daughter and schemed to evict him from, on the pretext that the place was a plague-spot, a rat's nest. The man Pasternak considered the greatest Russian stylist had come to that. The contrast between the wretched, withered old man, long forgotten by the world, and the image of the brilliant youth in front of me robbed me of any desire to visit the rest of the exhibition.

*

The Ancients mistrusted success because they feared not only the gods' jealousy but, even more, the danger of an inner imbalance linked to any success as such. To have understood this jeopardy — how far beyond us they were!

*

Impossible to spend sleepless nights and accomplish anything: if, in my youth, my parents had not *financed* my insomnias, I should surely have killed myself.

*

In 1849 Sainte-Beuve wrote that youth was turning away from *le mal romantique* in order to dream, like the Saint-Simonians, of "the limitless triumph of industry." This dream, which has come true, discredits all our undertakings, and the very idea of *hope*.

*

Those children I never wanted to have — if only they knew what happiness they owe me!

*

While my dentist was crushing my jaw, I realized that Time is the one subject for meditation, that because of Time I was in this fatal chair and everything was breaking down, including what was left of my teeth.

*

If I have always mistrusted Freud, my father is responsible: he used to tell my mother his dreams, thus spoiling all my mornings.

*

A hankering for evil is innate — no need to acquire it by effort. The child exercises his nasty instincts from the first — with what skill, what competence, and what rage! A pedagogy worthy of the name should prescribe sessions in a straitjacket. And perhaps, past childhood, we should extend this measure to every age, for the good of all concerned.

*

Woe to the writer who fails to cultivate his megalomania, who sees it diminished without taking action. He will soon discover that one does not become *normal* with impunity.

*

I was suffering from torments I could not dispel. A ring at the door; I opened it: a lady of a certain age whom I was certainly not expecting. For three hours she assailed me with such nonsense that my torments turned to rage. I was saved.

*

Tyranny destroys or strengthens the individual; freedom enervates him, until he becomes no more than a puppet. Man has more chances of saving himself by hell than by paradise.

*

Two friends, both actresses in a country of eastern Europe. One decamps to the West, becoming rich and famous there; the other remains where she is, poor and obscure. Half a century later, the second woman takes a trip and pays a visit to her fortunate colleague. "She used to be a head taller than me, and now she's a shrunken old woman, and paralyzed into the bargain." Other details follow, and in conclusion: "I'm not afraid of death; I'm afraid of death in life." Nothing like recourse to philosophical reflection to camouflage a belated revenge.

✳

Fragments, fugitive thoughts, you say. Can you call them *fugitive* when you are dealing with obsessions — with thoughts whose precise quality is not to *flee?*

✳

I had just written a very temperate, very correct note to someone who scarcely deserved it. Before sending it, I added a few allusions vaguely tinged with gall. And then, just when I was putting the thing in the mailbox, I felt myself clutched by rage and, along with it, by a disdain for my noble impulse, for my regrettable fit of *distinction.*

✳

Picpus Cemetery. A young man and a lady past her prime. The caretaker explains that this cemetery is reserved for descendants of those who were guillotined. The lady blurts out, "But that's who we are!" With what an expression! After all, she might have been telling the truth. Yet that provocative tone immediately put me on the executioner's side.

✳

Opening Meister Eckhart's *Sermons,* I read that suffering is intolerable to one who suffers for himself but light to one who suffers for God, because it is God who bears the burden, though it be heavy with the suffering of all mankind. It is no accident that I have come across this passage, for it perfectly applies to one who can never relieve himself of all that weighs upon him.

*

According to the kabbala, God permits His splendor to diminish so that men and angels can endure it — which comes down to saying that the Creation coincides with an impoverishment of the divine lumen, an effort toward darkness to which the Creator has assented. The hypothesis of God's deliberate obscuration has the merit of making us accessible to our own shadows, responsible for our irreceptivity to a certain light.

*

The ideal: to be able to repeat oneself like . . . Bach.

*

Immense, supernatural aridity: as if I were beginning a second existence on another planet where speech is unknown, in a universe refractory to language and incapable of creating such a thing for itself.

*

One does not inhabit a country; one inhabits a language. That is our country, our fatherland — and no other.

*

After reading in a work of psychoanalytic inspiration that as a young man Aristotle was jealous of Philip, the father of Alexander, his future pupil, one cannot help regarding a would-be therapeutic system in which such situations are posited as suspect, for it *invents* secrets for the pleasure of inventing explanations and cures.

*

There is something of the charlatan in anyone who triumphs in any realm whatever.

*

Visit a hospital, and in five minutes you become a Buddhist, or become one again if you have left off being such a thing.

*

Parmenides. Nowhere do I perceive the Being he exalts, and fail to see myself in his sphere, which includes no fault, no *place* for me.

*

In this compartment, a hideous woman sitting opposite, snoring, mouth open: an obscene agony. What was to be done? How endure such a spectacle? Stalin came to my aid. In his youth, passing between two rows of cossacks who were whipping him, he utterly concentrated upon reading a book, so that his consciousness of the blows was completely diverted. Strengthened by this example, I too plunged into my book, and halted at each word with extreme application till the moment the monster ended her agony.

*

I was saying to a friend the other day that while I no longer believed in "writing," I was reluctant to abandon it, that work was a defensible illusion, and that after scribbling a page or even a sentence, I always felt like whistling.

*

Religions, like the ideologies that have inherited their vices, are reduced to crusades against humor.

*

Every philosopher I've ever known, without exception, was "impulsive." This flaw of the West has marked the very ones who should be exempt from it.

*

To be like God and not like the gods, that is the goal of the true mystics, who aim too high to condescend to polytheism.

*

I am invited to a colloquium abroad, there being a need, apparently, for my vacillations. The skeptic-on-duty of a decaying world.

*

My habitation? I shall never know. True, one has no better knowledge of where God resides, for what is the sense of the expression "to reside in oneself" for those of us who lack any *basis*, both in and outside ourselves?

*

I abuse the word *God;* I use it often, too often. I employ it each time I touch an extremity and need a word to designate what comes *after*. I prefer God to the Inconceivable.

*

One work of piety declares that the inability to take sides is a sign one is not "enlightened by the divine light." In other words, irresolution, that total *objectivity*, is the road to perdition.

*

I infallibly discern a flaw in all those who are interested in the same things as myself. . . .

*

To have read through a work on old age solely because the author's photograph led me to do so. That mixture of rictus and entreaty, and that expression of grimacing stupor — what hype, what an endorsement!

*

"This world was not created according to the will of Life," it is said in the Ginza, a Gnostic text of a Mandaean sect in Mesopotamia. Remember this whenever you have no better argument to neutralize a disappointment.

*

After so many years, after a whole life, I saw her again. "Why are you crying?" I asked her immediately. "I'm not," she answered. And indeed she was not crying, she was smiling at me, but age having distorted her features, joy no longer found access to her face, on which one might also have read, "Whoever does not die young will regret it sooner or later."

*

A man who survives spoils his . . . biography. In the long run, the only destinies that can be regarded as fulfilled are obstructed ones.

*

We should bother our friends only for our burial. And even then . . . !

*

Boredom, with a bad reputation for frivolity, nonetheless allows us to glimpse the abyss from which issues the need for prayer.

*

"God has created nothing more odious to Himself than this world, and from the day He created it, He has not glanced at it again, so much does He loathe it." The Moslem mystic who wrote that, I don't know who it was, I shall never know this friend's name.

*

Undeniable trump card of the dying: being able to utter banalities without compromising themselves.

*

Retiring to the countryside after the death of his daughter, Tullia, Cicero, overwhelmed by grief, wrote letters of consolation to himself. A pity they have not been recovered and, still more, that such a therapeutics has not found favor! True, if it had been adopted, religions would long since have gone bankrupt.

*

A patrimony all our own: the hours when we have done nothing. . . . It is they that form us, that individualize us, that make us *dissimilar*.

*

A Danish psychoanalyst suffering from insistent migraine and who had undergone treatment with a colleague, to no effect, went to Freud, who cured him in several months. It was Freud himself who declared he had done so, and he was readily believed. A disciple, however inept, cannot fail to feel better after daily contact with his master. What better cure than to see the man whom one esteems most in the world taking such extended interest in your miseries! Few infirmities would not yield to such solicitude. Let us recall that the master had every quality of a founder of a sect, though disguised as a man of science. If he achieved cures, it was less by method than by *faith*.

*

"Old age is the most unexpected thing of all that happens to man," notes Trotsky a few years before his end. If, as a young man, he had had the exact, visceral intuition of this truth, what a miserable revolutionary he would have made!

*

Noble deeds are possible only in periods when self-irony is not yet rife.

*

It was his lot to fulfill himself only halfway. Everything

in him was *truncated:* his way of life, like his way of thinking. A man of fragments, himself a fragment.

*

Dreams, by abolishing time, abolish death. The deceased take advantage of them in order to importune us. Last night, there was my father. He was just as I have always known him, yet I had a moment's hesitation. Suppose it wasn't my father? We embraced in the Rumanian manner but, as always with him, without effusion, without warmth, without the demonstrativeness customary in an expansive people. It was because of that sober, icy kiss that I knew it was indeed my father. I woke up realizing that one resuscitates only as an intruder, as a dream-spoiler, and that such distressing immortality is the only kind there is.

*

Punctuality, a kind of "pathology of scruple." To be on time, I would be capable of committing a crime.

*

Above the pre-Socratics, one is occasionally inclined to set those heresiarchs whose works were mutilated or destroyed and who survive only in a few fragments of speech, as mysterious as one could wish for.

*

Why, after performing a good deed, does one long to follow a flag, any flag? Generous impulses involve a certain danger; they make one lose one's head — unless one is generous precisely because one has lost one's head already, generosity being a patent form of intoxication.

*

Each time the future seems conceivable to me, I have the impression of having been visited by Grace.

*

If only it were possible to identify that vice of fabrication whose trace the universe so visibly bears!

*

I am always amazed to see how lively, normal, and unassailable *low feelings* are. When you experience them, you feel cheered, restored to the community, on equal footing with your kind.

*

If man so readily forgets he is accursed, it is because he has always been so.

*

Criticism is a misconception: we must read not to understand others but to understand ourselves.

*

A man who sees himself *as he is* stands higher than a man who raises the dead, according to a saint. Not knowing oneself is the universal law, and no one transgresses it with impunity. The truth is that no one has the courage to transgress it, which accounts for the saint's exaggeration.

*

It is easier to imitate Jupiter than Lao-Tse.

*

Keeping up is the mark of a fluctuating mind that pursues nothing personal, that is unsuited to obsession, that *continual* impasse.

*

The eminent ecclesiastic sneered at Original Sin. "That sin is your livelihood. Without it you would starve to death, for your ministry would have no further meaning. If man has not fallen since his origins, why has Christ come? To redeem whom, and what?" To my objections, his sole response was a condescending smile. A religion is finished when only its adversaries strive to preserve its integrity.

*

The Germans do not see that it is absurd to put a Pascal and a Heidegger in the same bag. The abyss yawns between a *Schicksal* and a *Beruf,* between a destiny and a profession.

*

A sudden silence in the middle of a conversation suddenly brings us back to essentials: it reveals how dearly we must pay for the invention of speech.

*

To have nothing more in common with men than the fact of being a man!

*

A sensation must have fallen very low to deign to turn into an idea.

*

Believing in God dispenses one from believing in anything else — which is an estimable advantage. I have always envied those who believed in Him, though to believe oneself God seems easier to me than believing *in* God.

*

A word, once dissected, no longer signifies anything, is nothing. Like a body that, after the autopsy, is less than a corpse.

*

Each desire provokes in me a counterdesire, so that whatever I do, all that matters is what I have not done.

*

Sarvam anityam: All is transitory (Buddha). A formula one should repeat at every hour of the day, at the — admirable — risk of dying of it.

*

Some diabolic thirst keeps me from exposing my pact with breathing.

*

To lose sleep and to change language: two ordeals, one not dependent on oneself, the other deliberate. Alone, face to face with the nights and with words.

*

The healthy are not real. They have everything except *being* — which is uniquely conferred by uncertain health.

*

Of all the ancients, Epicurus may have been best at disdaining the mob — one more reason for celebrating him. What a notion, to place a clown like Diogenes in so lofty a niche! It is the Garden in question I should have haunted, and not the marketplace, nor — a fortiori — the tub. . . . (Yet Epicurus himself has disappointed me more than once: does he not call Theognis of Megara a fool for proclaiming it was better not to be born or, once born, to pass as soon as possible through the gates of Hades?)

*

"If I were assigned to classify human miseries," writes the young Tocqueville, "I should do so in this order: sickness, death, doubt." Doubt as scourge: I could never have put forth such an opinion, but I understand it as well as if I had uttered it myself — in another life.

*

"The end of humanity will come when everyone is like me," I declared one day in a fit I have no right to identify.

*

No sooner does the door close behind me than I exclaim, "What perfection in the parody of hell!"

*

"It is for the gods to come to me, not for me to go to them," Plotinus answered his disciple Amelius, who had sought to take him to a religious ceremony. In whom in the Christian world could we find a like quality of pride?

*

You had to let him talk on, talk about everything, and try to isolate the dazzling things that escaped him. It was a meaningless verbal eruption, with the histrionic and crazy gesticulations of a saint. To put yourself on his level, you had to divagate in his fashion, to utter sublime and incoherent sentences. A posthumous tête-à-tête, between impassioned ghosts.

*

At Saint-Séverin, listening to the organist play the *Art of the Fugue*, I kept saying to myself, over and over, "There is the *refutation* of all my anathemas."

2

Joseph de Maistre
An Essay on Reactionary Thought

∗

AMONG THINKERS — such as Nietzsche or Saint Paul — with the appetite and the genius for provocation, Joseph de Maistre occupies a place anything but negligible. Raising the most trivial problem to the level of paradox and the dignity of scandal, brandishing anathemas with enthusiastic cruelty, he created an oeuvre rich in enormities, a system that unfailingly seduces and exasperates. The scope and eloquence of his umbrage, the passion he devoted to indefensible causes, his tenacity in legitimizing one injustice after another, and his predilection for the deadly epithet make of him that immoderate disputant who, not deigning to persuade the adversary, crushes him with an adjective straight off. His convictions have an appearance of great firmness: he managed to overpower the solicitations of skepticism by the arrogance of his prejudices, by the dogmatic vehemence of his contempt.

Toward the end of the last century, at the height of the liberal illusion, it was possible to indulge in the luxury of calling him the "prophet of the past," of regarding him as a relic or an aberrant phenomenon. But we — in a somewhat more disabused epoch — know he is one of us precisely to the degree that he was a "monster"; it is in fact by the odious aspect of his "doctrines" that he *lives* for us, that he is our contemporary. Even if he were obsolete, moreover, he would still belong to that family of minds which date *incorruptibly*.

We must envy his luck, his privilege of disconcerting both admirers and detractors, of obliging either party to wonder: did he really produce an apology for the executioner and for war, or merely confine himself to acknowledging their necessity? In his indictment of Port-Royal, did he express what he really thought, or simply yield to a momentary impulse? Where does the theoretician leave off and the partisan begin? Was he a cynic, an enthusiast, or merely an aesthete who strayed into Catholicism?

To sustain the ambiguity, to confound us with convictions as clear-cut as his: this was certainly a tour de force. Inevitably readers began to question the authenticity of his fanaticism, to note the restrictions he himself set upon the brutality of his remarks, and insistently to cite his rare complicities with common sense. We ourselves shall not insult him by supposing him tepid. What attracts us is his pride, his marvelous insolence, his lack of equity, of proportion, and occasionally of decency. If he did not constantly irritate us, would we still have the patience to read him? The truths of which he made himself an apostle amount to something only by the impassioned distortion his temperament inflicted upon them. He transfigured the insipidities of the catechism and imparted to ecclesiastical commonplaces a flavor of extravagance. Religions die for lack of paradox: he knew this, or felt it, and in order to save Christianity, he contrived to inject it with a little more spice, a little more horror. Here he was aided much more by his talent as a writer than by his piety, which, in the opinion of Madame Swetchine, who knew him well, lacked any warmth whatever. Infatuated with corrosive expression, how could he stoop to the flabby phrases of the missal? (A pamphleteer at prayer? Conceivable, though hardly attractive.) Humility, a virtue alien to his nature, he pretends to only when he remembers that he must react *as a Christian.* Some of his exegetes have impugned — not without regret — his sincerity, whereas they ought to have relished the uneasiness he inspired: without his contradictions, without the misunderstandings that he — either by instinct or by design — created about himself, his case would have been dismissed long since, his career been closed, and his work suffered the misfortune of being understood, the worst fate that can befall an author.

A fusion of the acrimonious and the elegant in his genius and in his style evokes the image of an Old Testament prophet *and* of a man of the eighteenth century. In him inspiration and irony are no longer irreconcilable; he allows us to share — by his rages and his repartee — in the encounter of space and intimacy, infinity and the salon. But while he venerated the Bible to the point of admiring indiscriminately its treasures and its trivialities, he thoroughly hated the *Encyclopédie,* though he was attached to it by the form of his intelligence and the quality of his prose.

*   *   *

Imbued with a bracing rage, his books are never boring. In them we see him, paragraph by paragraph, immoderately exalt or disparage an idea, an event, an institution, adopting toward them the tone of a prosecutor or of a thurifer: "Any Frenchman who is a friend to the Jansenists is a fool or a Jansenist." "Everything in the French Revolution is miraculously bad." "The greatest enemy of Europe, a foe to be crushed by all means short of crime, the deadly cancer lodged in all sovereignties and unremittingly feeding on them, the son of pride, the father of anarchy, the universal dissolvent, is Protestantism." "In the first place, there is nothing so just, so learned, so incorruptible as the great Spanish tribunals, and if, to this general character, we add that of the Catholic priesthood, we shall be convinced, before any experience, that in all the universe there can be nothing more peaceful, more circumspect, more humane by nature than the tribunal of the Inquisition."

Ignorant of the practice of excess, we could learn it from de Maistre, who is as likely to compromise what he loves as what he loathes. A hoard of panegyrics, an avalanche of dithyrambic arguments, his book *Du Pape* somewhat disconcerted the Sovereign Pontiff, who realized the danger of such an apology. There is only one way to praise: to inspire fear in the figure being extolled, to compel him in fear and trembling to hide himself far away from the statue being erected, to constrain him by generous hyperbole to measure his mediocrity and suffer from it. What is an argument for the defense that neither torments nor troubles — what is a eulogy that fails to kill? Every apology should be a murder by enthusiasm.

*   *   *

"There exists no great character that does not tend to some exaggeration," de Maistre writes, doubtless thinking of himself. We may note that the decisive and often frenzied tone of his works is not to be discerned in his letters; these caused amazement when they were published: who could have suspected such amenity in the raging doctrinaire? The reaction of surprise, which was unanimous, strikes us as a trifle naive. After all, a thinker generally puts his madness into his works and keeps his common sense for his ordinary relations; he will always be more pitiless and unbridled when he attacks a theory than when he must address a friend or an acquaintance. Intimacy with an idea incites to delirium, obliterates judgment, and produces the illusion of omnipotence. In truth, the tête-à-tête with ideas generates madness, deprives the mind of its equilibrium and pride of its composure. Our excesses and our aberrations derive from our combat with unrealities, with abstractions, from our will to triumph over what does not exist — whence the impure, tyrannical, wandering aspect of philosophical works, moreover of any work at all. The thinker blackening a page without recipient believes — feels! — himself to be the arbiter of the world. Yet in his letters he expresses, on the contrary, his hopes, his weaknesses, his defeats; he attenuates the audacities of his books and rests from his excesses. De Maistre's correspondence was that of a moderate man. Some, delighted to find a different writer, quickly classified him among the liberals, forgetting that he was tolerant in his life only because he was anything but in his works, where the best pages are precisely those in which he magnifies the abuses of the Church and the rigors of the State.

Had it not been for the Revolution, which, wresting him from his habitual preoccupations — indeed, crushing him — awakened him to the great problems, he would have lived, in Chambéry, the life of a good paterfamilias and a good Freemason, continuing to dose his Catholicism, his royalism, and his Martinism with that tincture of Rousseauist phraseology which mars his early writings. The French army, invading Savoy, drove him out; he took the road of exile; thereby his mind profited, and his style as well, as we discover when we compare his *Considérations sur la France* with the declamatory and diffuse productions antedating the revolutionary period. Disaster, clarifying his prejudices and his tastes, saved him from vagueness while rendering him forever incapable of serenity and objectivity, virtues rare in the émigré. De .Maistre was one of these, and precisely during those years (1803–1817) when he served as the King of Sardinia's ambassador to St. Petersburg. All his thoughts were to bear the mark of exile: "There is only violence in the universe; but we are deceived by modern philosophy, which asserts that all is for the best, whereas the worst has corrupted everything, and in a very real sense, all is for the worst, since nothing is where it belongs."

"Nothing is where it belongs": the refrain of all emigrations, and also the point of departure for all philosophical reflection. The mind wakens upon contact with disorder and injustice: whatever is "where it belongs," whatever is normal, leaves the mind indifferent, benumbed, while frustration and dispossession enhance and animate it. A thinker is enriched by all that escapes him, all that is taken from him; if he should happen to lose his country, what a windfall! Thus the exile is a thinker in miniature or a circumstantial visionary, tossed between hope and fear, on the lookout for events he longs for or dreads. If he has genius, he rises above them, like de

Maistre, and interprets them: "The first condition of a decreed revolution is that everything that might have forestalled it does not exist, and that those who seek to prevent it must fail entirely. But order is never more apparent, Providence is never more palpable, than when a higher action takes man's place and operates in and of itself: this is what we are seeing at this moment."

In periods when we become aware of the nullity of our initiatives, we identify destiny either with Providence — a reassuring disguise for fatality, a camouflage of failure, an admission of our impotence to organize the future, yet a desire to discern its essential contours and determine their meaning — or with a mechanical, impersonal play of forces, the automatism of which controls our actions and even our beliefs. Yet we invest this play of forces, however impersonal and mechanical, with a glamour that its very definition forbids, and we relate it — a conversion of concepts into universal agents — to a moral power responsible for events and the turn they must take. At the height of positivism, did we not invoke, in mystical terms, a Future to which we attributed an energy scarcely less effective than that of Providence? Inveterately there slips into our explanations a wisp of theology, inherent in, even indispensable to, our thought insofar as it undertakes to provide a coherent image of the world.

To attribute a meaning to the historical process, even one derived from a logic immanent to the future, is to subscribe, more or less explicitly, to a form of Providence. Bossuet, Hegel, and Marx, by the very fact that they assign a meaning to events, belong to the same family or at least do not essentially differ from each other, the important thing being not to define or determine this meaning but to resort to it, to postulate it; and they resort to it, they postulate it. To turn from a theological or metaphysical conception to historical materialism is simply to change providentialisms. Were we in the habit of looking beyond the specific content of ideologies and doctrines, we should see that to claim kinship with one of them rather than some other does not at all imply much expenditure of sagacity. Those following one party imagine they differ from those following another, whereas all, once they choose, join each other *underneath,* participate in one and the same nature, and vary only in appearance, by the mask they assume. It is folly to imagine that truth resides in choice, when any adoption of a position is equivalent to a contempt for truth. To our misfortune, choice, position-taking, is a fatality no one escapes; each of us must opt for a nonreality, an error, obligatory fanatics that we are, sick men, fever victims: our assents, our adherences, are so many alarming symptoms. Whoever identifies himself with anything gives evidence of morbid dispositions: no salvation and no health outside of pure being — as pure as the Void. But let us return to Providence, a subject scarcely less vague. To discover how seriously a historical period was stricken, the dimensions of the disaster it was obliged to suffer, simply measure the desperation with which believers justified the designs, the program, and the behavior of the divinity. Not at all surprising that de Maistre's crucial work, *Les Soirées de Saint-Pétersbourg,* should be a variation on the theme of the temporal government of Providence: did he not live in a time when making his contemporaries discern the effects of divine goodness required the combined resources of sophistry, faith, and illusion? In the fifth century, in a Gaul ravaged by barbarian invasions, Salvianus, writing *De Guberna-tione Dei,* had faced a similar task: desperate combat against the evidence, mission without an object, intellectual effort based on hallucination. . . . Justification by Providence is the quixotism of theology.

Dependent though it is on various historical moments, a sensibility to fate is nonetheless conditioned by the nature of the individual. Whoever engages in important enterprises knows himself to be at the mercy of a reality that is beyond him. Only frivolous minds, only the "irresponsible," believe they act freely; the rest, at the heart of an essential experience, are rarely free from the obsession of necessity or of their "star." Rulers are administrators of Providence, observes Saint-Martin; elsewhere, Friedrich Meinecke remarks that in Hegel's system, heroes figure as no more than functionaries of Absolute Spirit. An analogous sentiment led de Maistre to call the leaders of the Revolution merely "automata," "instruments," "villains," who, far from governing events, on the contrary submitted to their course.

As for these automata, these instruments, how were they more culpable than the "higher" power that had provoked them and whose decrees they were so faithfully executing? Would that power not be equally "villanous"? Since it represented for de Maistre the only fixed point in the midst of the revolutionary "whirlwind," he does not indict it, or at least he behaves as if he accepted its sovereignty without argument. In his mind, it would in fact intervene only at moments of disturbance and would vanish during periods of calm, so that he implicitly identifies it with a temporal phenomenon, with a circumstantial Providence, useful in explaining catastrophes, superfluous in the intervals between them and when passions die down. For us it is fully justified only if manifest everywhere and always, only if it keeps permanent vigil. What was such a power doing before 1789? Was it sleeping? Was it not at its post throughout the eighteenth century, and did it not want anything to do with that century which de Maistre, despite his theory of divine intervention, makes chiefly responsible for the advent of the guillotine?

For him such a power assumes a content, becomes truly Providence, starting from a miracle, from the Revolution; ". . . that in the dead of winter a man should command a tree, in the presence of a thousand witnesses, suddenly to cover itself with leaves and fruit, and that the tree should obey, everyone will acclaim as a miracle and hail the thaumaturge. But the French Revolution and all that is happening at this moment is quite as wondrous, in its way, as the instantaneous fructification of a tree in the month of January."

Facing a force that performs such marvels, the believer will wonder how to safeguard his freedom, how to avoid the temptation of quietism and the more serious one of fatalism. Such difficulties, raised early in the *Considérations,* the author attempts to evade by subtleties or by equivocation: "We are all attached to the throne of the Supreme Being by a supple chain that binds but does not enslave us. What is admirable in the universal order of things is the action of free beings under the divine hand. Freely enslaved, they function at once by will and by necessity: they really do as they wish, but without being able to upset the general plan."

*   *   *

"A supple chain," slaves who act "freely": these are incompatibilities that betray the thinker's embarrassment over the impossibility of reconciling divine omnipotence and human freedom. And it is doubtless in order to save that freedom, to leave it a wider field of action, that he postulates the withdrawal of divine intervention in moments of equilibrium — brief intervals indeed, for Providence, reluctant to remain long in eclipse, emerges from its repose only to strike, to manifest its severity. War will be its "department," in which it permits man to act "only in a virtually mechanical fashion, since successes in this realm depend almost entirely upon what depends least upon him." War will therefore be "divine," "a law of the world" — divine above all in the way it breaks out: "At the very moment occasioned by men and prescribed by justice, God advances to avenge the iniquity that the inhabitants of the world have committed against Him."

Divine: there is no adjective de Maistre uses more readily. Constitution, sovereignty, hereditary monarchy, and papacy are all, according to him, "divine" institutions, as is any authority consolidated by tradition, any order whose origins data back to a remote period; the rest is all "wretched usurpation," hence "human" work. In short, *divine* relates to the body of institutions and phenomena execrated by liberal thought. Applied to war, the adjective seems, at first glance, unfortunate; replace it with *irrational* and it is no longer so. This kind of substitution, if made in many of de Maistre's observations, would attenuate their scandalous character; but by resorting to it, do we not ultimately dilute a thought whose virulence constitutes its charm? The fact remains that to name and invoke God at every moment, to associate Him with the horrible, has something about it that sends chills down the spine of any balanced, reticent, and reasonable believer, contrary to the fanatic — the real believer — who relishes the divinity's bloodthirsty escapades.

Divine or not, war, as it is treated in the *Soirées,* does not fail to exert a certain fascination upon us. This ceases to be true when it obsesses a second-order mind such as de Maistre's Spanish disciple, Donoso Cortès: "War, God's work, is good, as all His works are good; but a war can be disastrous and unjust, because it is the work of man's free will." "I have never been able to understand those who anathematize war. Such anathema is contrary to philosophy and to religion; those who pronounce it are neither philosophers nor Christians."

The master's thought, already established in an extreme position, scarcely tolerates the additional exaggeration afforded by the pupil. Bad causes require talent or temperament. The disciple, by definition, possesses neither.

In de Maistre, aggression is inspiration; hyperbole, innate knowledge. Carried to extremes, he dreams of nothing better than taking us with him. And so he manages to reconcile us to war, as he reconciles us to the executioner's solitude, if not to the executioner himself. Christian by persuasion rather than by sentiment, quite alien to the figures of the New Testament, he secretly loves the pomp of intolerance, and it suits him to be intractable: is is for nothing that he grasped so thoroughly the spirit of the Revolution? And would he have managed to describe its vices had he not recognized them in himself? As an enemy of the Terror — and one never opposes with impunity an

event, an epoch, or an idea — he would have to combat
it by steeping himself in it, assimilating it. His religious
experience would be marked thereby: the obsession with
blood prevails. Hence he is more attracted by the old God
("the God of hosts") than by Christ, whom he always
mentions in conventional, "sublime" phrases, and usually
to justify the theory — interesting, though no more than
that — of the reversibility of the sufferings of the innocent
to the advantage of the guilty. Moreover, the only Christ
who might have suited him is the figure of Spanish sculp-
ture, sanguinolent, disfigured, convulsive, and pleased to
the point of delirium by His crucifixion.

By packing God off, outside of the world and human
affairs, by dispossessing Him of the virtues and faculties
that would have allowed Him to make His presence and
His authority felt, the deists had reduced Him to the level
of an idea and a symbol, an abstract figuration of goodness and wisdom. After a century of "philosophy," the
point was to restore His ancient privileges, the status of
tyrant that had been stripped from Him· so pitilessly.
Good, correct, He had ceased to be fearsome, losing all
empire over men's minds — an enormous danger, of
which de Maistre was more conscious than any of his
contemporaries and which he could rout only by insisting
on the reestablishment of the "true" God, the terrible
one. We understand nothing about religions if we suppose
that man flees a capricious, wicked, and even ferocious
divinity, or if we forget that he loves fear to the point of
frenzy.

The problem of Evil actually troubles only a few sensitive souls, a few skeptics, repelled by the way in which

the believer comes to terms with it or spirits it away.
Hence it is to these that theodicies are primarily addressed,
attempts to humanize God, frantic acrobatics that collapse
and compromise themselves on this ground, constantly belied as they are by experience. Try as they will to be per-
suasive, they fail; they are declared suspect, incriminated,
and asked for accountings, in the name of one piece of
evidence — Evil — evidence that a de Maistre will attempt
to deny. "Everything is Evil," he instructs us; yet Evil, he
hastens to add, comes down to a "purely negative" force
that has nothing "in common with existence," comes
down to a "schism in being," to an accident. Others will
assert on the contrary that quite as constitutive of being
as Good, and quite as real, Evil is nature, an essential in-
gredient of existence and anything but an accessory phenomenon, and that the problems Evil raises become
insoluble as soon as we refuse to introduce it into the composition of the divine substance. Just as sickness is not an
absence of health but a reality as positive and as lasting
as health, in the same way Evil is worth as much as Good,
even exceeds it in indestructibility and plenitude. Good
and Evil principles coexist and mingle in God, as they coexist and mingle in the world. The notion of God's cul-
pability is not a gratuitous one, but necessary and
perfectly compatible with the notion of His omnipotence:
only such an idea confers some intelligibility on the historical process, on all it contains that is monstrous, mad,
and absurd. To attribute goodness and purity to the creator of becoming is to abandon all comprehension of the
majority of events, especially the most important one: the
Creation. God could not avoid the influence of Evil,
mainspring of actions, an agent indispensable to Whoever,
exasperated by self-containment, aspires to emerge, to

spread Himself and corrupt Himself in time. If Evil, the secret of our dynamism, were to withdraw from our lives, we should vegetate in that monotonous perfection of the Good which, according to Genesis, vexed Being itself. The combat between the two principles, Good and Evil, is waged on every level of existence, including eternity. We are plunged into the adventure of the Creation, one of the most dreadful of exploits, without "moral purposes" and perhaps without meaning; and though the idea and the initiative for it are God's, we cannot reproach him for it, so great in our eyes is His prestige as the first guilty party. By making us His accomplices, He associated us with that vast movement of solidarity in Evil which sustains and affirms the universal confusion.

No doubt de Maistre would not participate in a doctrine grounded in reason to this degree: does he not propose to lend some versimilitude to so audacious a theory as that of a divinity essentially and uniquely good? A difficult, even an unrealizable enterprise, which he hopes to bring off by overwhelming human nature: ". . . no man is punished as just, but always as a man, so that it is untrue to say that virtue suffers in this world: it is human nature that suffers, and that always deserves to do so."

How can we require of the just man that he separate his quality as a man from his quality as just? No innocent person will go so far as to assert, "I am suffering as a man, not as a good man." To propose such a dissociation is to commit a psychological error, is to be deceived as to the meaning of Job's rebellion and not to understand that the plague-stricken man yielded to God less out of conviction than out of weariness. Nothing permits us to regard goodness as the major attribute of the divinity. De Maistre himself sometimes seems tempted to think as much. "What is an injustice of God with regard to man? Do you suppose there is some common legislator above God who has prescribed how He must act toward man? And what will be the nature of such a judge between Him and ourselves?" "The more terrible God seems to us, the more we must redouble our religious fear of Him, the more ardent and indefatigable our prayers must become: for there is no vindication that His goodness will suffice." And he adds, in one of the most significant passages of the *Soirées,* these indiscreet considerations: "Since the proof of God precedes that of His attributes, we know *that* He is before knowing *what* He is. Thus we find ourselves in an empire whose sovereign has published once and for all the laws that rule the world. These laws are, in general, marked with the striking signs of wisdom and even of goodness; yet some (I suppose) seem harsh, even unjust; whereupon I ask all the malcontents, what should be done? Depart from the empire, perhaps? Impossible: it is everywhere, and nothing is outside it. Complain, sulk, write against the sovereign? Only to be thrashed or put to death. There is no better side to take than that of resignation and respect, I may even say of love; for, since we start from the supposition that the Master exists, and that He must absolutely be served, is it not better (whatever He be) to serve Him with love than without love?"

An unhoped-for avowal that would have delighted a Voltaire. Providence is unmasked, denounced, rendered suspect, by the very man who had put himself forward to celebrate its goodness, its honorable character. Admirable sincerity, the dangers of which de Maistre must have understood. Subsequently he will forget himself less and less and, as usual, returning the focus to man, will abandon the inculpation of God by rebellion, jeers, or despair. The better to reproach human nature for the evils it endures, he will forget that eminently untenable theory of the moral origin of diseases. "If there were no moral evil upon earth, there would be no physical evil"; ". . . all suffering is a torment imposed for some crime, present or original"; "if I have made no distinction among diseases, it is because they are all punishments."

This doctrine he derives from that of Original Sin, without which, he tells us, "one explains nothing." But he is mistaken when he reduces Sin to a primitive transgression, to a concerted and immemorial fault, instead of seeing in it a flaw, a vice of nature; he is also mistaken when, after speaking correctly of an "original disease," he attributes it to our iniquities, whereas it is, like Sin, inscribed in our very essence: primordial disorder, calamity affecting good and wicked, virtuous and vicious alike.

As long as he confines himself to describing the ills that overwhelm us, de Maistre is veracious; he strays from truth when he tries to explain and justify their distribution on earth. His observations seem to us exact; his theories and his value judgments, inhuman and erroneous. If, as he likes to think, diseases are punishments, then the hospitals are crammed with monsters and the incurable are by far the greatest criminals in existence. Let us not take apologetics to its ultimate position; let us show some indulgence with regard to those who, eager to disinculpate God, to put Him above suspicion, reserve to man alone the honor of having conceived Evil. . . . Like all great ideas, that of the Fall accounts for everything and for nothing, and it is quite as difficult to utilize as it is to do without. But finally, whether the Fall can be imputed to a fault or a fatality, to an action of moral order or to a metaphysical principle, the fact remains that it explains, at least in part, our erring ways, our inconclusiveness, our fruitless quests, the terrible singularity of beings, the role of disturber, of broken-down and inventive animal, that was assigned to each of us. And if it involves a number of points subject to caution, there is one, however, whose importance is incontestable: the one that traces our failure to our separation from the All. It could not escape de Maistre: "The more one examines the universe, the more one is inclined to believe that Evil proceeds from a certain division that cannot be explained, and that the return to Good depends on a contrary force that ceaselessly impels us toward a unity just as inconceivable."

How to explain such division? Attribute it to the insinuation of Becoming within Being? To the infiltration of movement into the primordial unity? To a fatal shock given to the happy indistinction before there was time? Who knows? What seems certain is that "history" proceeds from a broken identity, from an initial laceration, source of the multiple, source of Evil.

The notion of Sin, associated with that of division, satisfies the mind only if used with caution, instead of in de Maistre's fashion, for he quite arbitrarily proceeds to imagine a *second-order* Original Sin, responsible, he says, for the existence of the savage, that "descendant of a man detached from the great tree of civilization by an ordinary prevarication," a fallen being who cannot be regarded

"without reading the anathema written, I am not saying
merely in his soul, but even upon the external form of his
body," "stricken in the last depths of his moral essence,"
not at all like primitive man, for "with our intelligence,
our morality, our sciences, and our arts, we are precisely
to primitive man what the savage is to us."

And our author, quick to hurl himself to the extremities
of an idea, maintains that "the state of civilization and of
knowledge in a certain sense is the natural and primitive
state of man," that the first humans, "marvelous" beings,
having begun with a knowledge higher than ours, perceived the effects in the causes and found themselves in
possession of "precious communications" dispensed by
"beings of a higher order," and that moreover certain peoples refractory to our mode of thought seem still to preserve the memory of "primitive knowledge" and of "the
era of intuition."

Thus we find civilization placed before history! This
idolatry of beginnings, of a paradise already realized, this
obsession with origins, is the very sign of "reactionary"
or, if one prefers, "traditional" thought. We can certainly
conceive of an "era of intuition," yet only on condition
that we do not identify it with civilization itself, which —
in a break with the mode of intuitive knowledge — supposes complex relations between being and knowing, as
well as man's inaptitude for emerging from his own categories, a "civilized" person being by definition alien to
essence, to the simultaneous perception of the immediate
and the ultimate. It is playing with words to speak of a
perfect civilization before the appearance of the conditions
capable of making any civilization possible; we abusively

enlarge the concept of civilization if we include the golden age within it. History, according to de Maistre, will bring us back — by the detour of Evil and Sin — to the unity of the paradisal age, to the "perfect" civilization, to the secrets of "primitive knowledge." What those secrets consisted of, we shall not be so indiscreet as to ask him: he has declared them impenetrable, the prerogative of "marvelous" men, no less impenetrable than they. De Maistre never offers a hypothesis without immediately treating it with all the considerations due to certainty; how could he doubt the existence of an immemorial knowledge when without it he could not "explain" to us the very first of all our catastrophes? The punishments being proportional to the guilty party's knowledge, the Flood, he assures us, presupposes "unheard-of crimes," and these crimes presuppose in their turn "knowledge infinitely superior to that which we possess." A lovely and improbable theory, comparable to the one about savages, of which these are the terms: "A leader of a people having diluted the moral principle among them by a number of those prevarications which, to all appearances, are no longer possible in the present state of affairs because we fortunately no longer know enough to become guilty to this degree — this leader, then, transmitted the anathema to his posterity; and any constant force being by its nature accelerative, since it continually adds to itself, such degradation weighing continually upon the descendants has ultimately made them into what we call savages."

No clue as to the nature of this prevarication. We shall know little more about it when we are told that it is imputable to an Original Sin of the second order. Is it not too convenient, in order to whitewash Providence, to ascribe to the creature alone the anomalies which abound on earth? If man is degraded in principle, his degradation, like that of the savage, cannot have begun with a sin committed at a given moment — by a prevarication invented, by and large, to consolidate a system and sustain a cause, both highly dubious.

The doctrine of the Fall makes a powerful appeal to reactionaries of whatever stripe; the most hardened and the most lucid among them know, moreover, what recourse it offers against the glamour of revolutionary optimism: does it not postulate the invariability of human nature, irremediably doomed to corruption and collapse? Consequently there is no way out, no solution to the conflicts that desolate societies nor any possibility of a radical change that might modify their structure: history, identical time, context for the monotonous process of our degradation! Invariably the reactionary, that conservative who has dropped the mask, will borrow the worst of traditional wisdom, and the most profound: the conception of the irreparable, the static vision of the world. All wisdom and a fortiori all metaphysics are reactionary, as becomes any form of thought that, seeking constants, emancipates itself from the superstition of the diverse and the possible. Contradiction in terms: a revolutionary sage, or a revolutionary metaphysician. At a certain degree of attachment and clear-sightedness, history has no further value, man himself ceases to count: to break with appearances is to vanquish action and the illusions deriving from it. When you stress the essential misery of beings, you do not stop at the one that results from social inequalities, nor do you strive to remedy them. (Can we imagine a revolution drawing its slogans from Pascal?)

*   *   *

Often the reactionary is merely a cunning, an *interested* sage who, politically exploiting the great metaphysical truths, examines without weakness or pity the underside of the human phenomenon in order to broadcast its horror — a profiteer of the terrible whose thought, paralyzed by calculation or by an excess of lucidity, minimizes or calumniates time. More generous (being more naive), revolutionary thought, on the other hand, associating the erosion of Becoming with the notion of substantiality, discerns in succession a principle of enrichment, a fruitful dislocation of identity and monotony, and a sort of continuous perfectibility. A challenge hurled at the notion of Original Sin: such is the ultimate meaning of revolutions. Before liquidating the established order, they seek to release man from the worship of origins to which religion condemns him; they do so only by undermining the gods, by weakening their power over men's minds. For it is the gods who, by binding us to a world before history, make us scorn Becoming, that fetish of all innovators, from the simple grumbler to the anarchist.

Our political conceptions are dictated to us by our sentiment, or our vision, of time. If eternity haunts us, what do we care about the changes taking place in the life of institutions or of peoples? To be interested in them, we must believe, with the revolutionary spirit, that time contains the potential answer to all questions and the remedy to all evils, that its unfolding involves the elucidation of mystery and the reduction of our perplexities, that time is the agent of a total metamorphosis. But here is the most curious thing of all: the revolutionary idolizes Becoming only up to the instauration of the order for which he fought; *subsequently,* for him, appears the ideal conclusion of time, the Forever of utopias, an extratemporal, unique, and infinite moment, provoked by the advent of a new age, entirely different from the others, an eternity here on earth that closes and crowns the historical process. The notion of a golden age, the notion of paradise *tout court,* pursues believers and unbelievers alike. However, between the primordial paradise of religions and the ultimate one of utopias, there is the interval separating regret from hope, remorse from illusion, perfection achieved from perfection unrealized. On which side effectiveness and dynamism may be found, we realize readily enough: the more specifically a moment is marked by the utopian spirit (which can very well assume a "scientific" disguise), the more chances it has of triumphing and of lasting. As the fortune of Marxism testifies, one always wins, on the level of action, by placing the absolute within the possible, not at the beginning but at the end of time. Like all reactionaries, de Maistre situated it in the past. The adjective *satanic,* which he applied to the French Revolution, he might just as well have extended to all events: his hatred of any innovation is equivalent to a hatred of movement as such. What he wants is to nail men to tradition, to deflect them from their need to question the value and the legitimacy of dogmas and institutions. "If He has placed certain objects beyond the limits of our vision, it is doubtless because it would be dangerous for us to perceive them clearly"; "I daresay what we should not know is more important than what we should know."

Positing that without the inviolability of mystery, order collapses, de Maistre counters the indiscretions of the critical spirit with the bans of orthodoxy, the multiplication of heresies, the rigor of a unique truth. But he goes too far, he begins raving, when he seeks to convince us that "any metaphysical proposition that does not self-evidently emerge from a Christian dogma is and can only be a cul- pable extravagance." A fanatic of obedience, he accuses the Revolution of having laid bare the basis of authority and of having revealed its secret to the uninitiated, to the mob. "If you give a child one of those toys which perform movements, inexplicable to him, by means of an internal mechanism, after having played with it for a moment, he will break it to see what's inside. It is thus that the French have treated their government. They have wanted to see inside; they have laid bare the political principles, they have opened the mob's eyes to objects that it had never occurred to them to examine, without realizing that there are things that are destroyed by being shown."

Remarks of an insolent, an aggressive lucidity, which might be made by the representative of any regime, of any party. Yet no liberal (nor any "man of the left") would ever dare to adopt them. Must authority, to maintain it- self, rest upon some mystery, some irrational foundation? the "right" says as much; the "left" denies it. A purely ideological difference; in fact, any order that seeks *to last* succeeds in doing so only by surrounding itself with a cer- tain obscurity, by flinging a veil over its motives and its actions, by generating an aura of the "sacred" that renders it impenetrable to the masses. This is an obvious fact that the "democratic" governments cannot adopt but that, on the other hand, is proclaimed by the reactionaries, who, unconcerned by public opinion and the consent of the crowd, shamelessly offer unpopular truisms, inoppor- tune banalities. By these the "democrats" are scandal- ized, though they know that "reaction" often translates their hidden thoughts, that it expresses certain of their innermost disappointments, many bitter certitudes of which they can give no public account. Committed to their "generous" program, they may not parade the slightest contempt for the "people," nor even for human nature; not having the right or the luck to invoke Original Sin, they must cajole and flatter man, must seek to "liberate" him: optimists sick at heart, anguished amid their fervors and their dreams, at once swept away and paralyzed by a uselessly noble, uselessly pure idea. How many times, in their heart of hearts, must they not envy the doctrinal offhandedness of their enemies! The leftist's despair is to do battle in the name of principles that forbid him cynicism.

Such torment was spared a de Maistre, who, dreading above all things the liberation of the individual, was careful to found authority on bases solid enough to resist the "dissolving" principles promulgated by the Reformation and the *Encyclopédie*. The better to affirm the notion of order, he will attempt to minimize the share of premeditation and of will in the creation of laws and institutions; he will deny that languages themselves have been invented, while conceding that they may have *begun;* nonetheless speech precedes man, for, he adds, it is only possible by the Word. The political meaning of such a doctrine is revealed to us by Bonald in the *Discours préliminaire* of his *Législation primitive*. If the human race has received speech, it has necessarily received with it "the knowledge of moral truth." Hence there exists a sovereign, fundamental law, as well as an order of duties and truths. "But if man, on the contrary, has made his speech himself, he has made his thought, he has made his law, he has made society, he has made everything and can destroy everything, and it is right that in the same party that asserts that speech is of human institution, society is regarded as an arbitrary convention. . . ."

Theocracy, ideal of reactionary thought, is based on both contempt for and fear of man, on the notion that he is too corrupt to deserve freedom, that he does not know how to use it, and that when it is granted him, he uses it against himself, so that in order to remedy his failure, laws and institutions must be made to rest on a transcendent principle, preferably on the authority of the old "terrible God," always ready to intimidate and discourage revolutions.

The new theocracy will be haunted by the old: the legislation of Moses is the only one, if we follow de Maistre, to have withstood time, it alone emerges "from the circle drawn around human power"; Bonald, for his part, will see in it "the strongest of all legislations," since it has produced the most "stable" people, destined to preserve the "deposit of all truths." If the Jews owe their civil rehabilitation to the Revolution, it devolved upon the Restoration to reconsider their religion and their past, to exalt their sacerdotal civilization, which Voltaire had flouted.

The Christian seeking the antecedents of his God quite naturally comes up against Jehovah; thus the fate of Israel intrigues him. The interest our two thinkers took in Israel was not, however, exempt from political calculations. This "stable" people, supposedly hostile to the craving for innovation that dominated the age — what a reproach to the fickle nations oriented toward modern ideas! A transient enthusiasm: when de Maistre realized that the Jews in Russia, faithless toward their theocratic tradition, were echoing certain ideologies imported from France, he turned against them, calling them subversive spirits and — the depth of abomination in his eyes — comparing them to Protestants. One dares not imagine the invectives reserved for them had he foreseen the role they were later to play in the movements of social emancipation, as much in Russia as in Europe. Too concerned by Moses' tablets, de Maistre could not anticipate those of Marx. . . . His affinities with the spirit of the Old Testament were so deep that his Catholicism seems, so to speak, Judaic, imbued with that prophetic frenzy of which he found but a faint trace in the gentle mediocrity of the Gospels. Tormented by the demon of vaticination, he sought everywhere signs heralding the return to Unity, the final triumph of . . . origins, the end of the process of degradation inaugurated by Evil and Sin; signs that obsess him to the point where he forgets God for them, or ponders Him to penetrate His manifestations rather than His nature, not Being but its reflections; and these appearances by which God is manifested are called Providence — sightings, ways, artifices of the alarming, the unspeakable divine strategy.

Because the author of the *Soirées* constantly invokes "mystery," because he reverts to it every time his reason comes up against some impassable frontier, readers have insisted, despite the evidence, on his mysticism, whereas the true mystic, far from questioning himself upon mystery, or diminishing it to a problem, or making use of it as a means of explanation, on the contrary settles himself within it from the start, is inseparable from it, and lives inside it as one lives inside a reality, his God not being, like that of the prophets, absorbed by time, traitor to eternity, entirely external and superficial, but indeed that God of our soliloquies and our lacerations, the deep God in Whom our outcries gather.

De Maistre, evidently, has opted for the God of the prophets — a "sovereign" God it is vain to rail against or be offended by, a churchwarden God uninterested in souls — just as he had opted for an abstract mystery, annex of theology or dialectics, a concept rather than an experience. Indifferent to the encounter of human solitude and divine solitude, much more accessible to the problems of religion than to the dramas of faith, inclined to establish between God and ourselves relations that are juridical rather than confidential, he increasingly emphasizes the laws (does he not speak as a magistrate of the mystery?) and reduces religion to a simple "cement of the political edifice," to the social function it fulfills — a hybrid synthesis of utilitarian preoccupations and theocratic inflexibility, a baroque mélange of fictions and dogmas. If he preferred the Father to the Son, he will prefer the Pope to either — by which I mean that, practical-minded in spite of everything, he will reserve for their delegate the most brilliant of his flatteries. "He has suffered a Catholic stroke": this witticism to which he was inspired by Werner's conversion suits de Maistre as well, for it is not God who has stricken him but a certain form of religion, an institutional expression of the absolute. A similar stroke had also affected Bonald, a thinker chiefly concerned with constructing a system of political theology. In a letter of July 18, 1818, de Maistre wrote to him, "Is it possible, Monsieur, that nature has entertained herself by putting two strings as perfectly in tune as your mind and mine! It is the most rigorous unison, a unique phenomenon!" One regrets this conformity of views with a lusterless and

deliberately limited writer — of whom Joubert once remarked, "He's a squireen of great wit and great knowledge, erecting his first prejudices into doctrines" — but
ultimately it sheds a certain light on the direction de
Maistre's thought was taking, as on the discipline he had
imposed upon himself in order to avoid risk and subjec-
tivism in matters of faith. Yet from time to time the visionary in him triumphs over the theologian's scruples
and, wresting him from the Pope and the rest, raises him
to the perception of eternity: "Occasionally I should like
to hurl myself beyond the narrow limits of this world; I
would like to anticipate the day of revelations and plunge
into the infinite. When the double law of man will be
erased and these two centers united, he will be ONE: no
longer having a war within, how would he have any idea
of duality? But if we consider men, comparing them with
each other, what will become of them when, Evil being
annihilated, there will be no more passion or personal
commitment? What will the Self become when all
thoughts will be common, like all desires, when all minds
will see each other as they are seen? Who can understand,
who can represent to himself, that heavenly Jerusalem,
where all the inhabitants, penetrated by the same spirit,
will penetrate one another, and each reflect the other's
happiness?"

"What will the Self become?": this concern is not that
of a mystic, for whom the self, precisely, is a nightmare
he intends to be rid of by vanishing into God, where he
knows the ecstasy of unity, object and end of his quest.
De Maistre seems never to have attained unity by sensation, by the leap of ecstasy, by that intoxication in which
the contours of being dissolve; for him unity remained the

obsession of a theoretician. Attached to that "self" of his, he had difficulty imagining the "heavenly Jerusalem," the return to a blessed pre-division identity, as well as that nostalgia for paradise he must nonetheless have experienced, if only as a limit-state. In order to conceive how such nostalgia can constitute an everyday experience, we must consider a figure by whom de Maistre was strongly influenced, that Claude de Saint-Martin who admitted to possessing only two things or, to use his own words, two "posts": paradise and the dust. "In 1817 I saw an old man in England named Best, who had the faculty of quoting, to anyone he met, very appropriate passages of Scripture without his ever having known you before. Upon seeing me, he began by saying, 'He has cast the world behind him.' " In a period of triumphant ideology, when the rehabilitation of man was noisily undertaken, no one was so deeply anchored in the Beyond as Saint-Martin, nor more qualified to preach the Fall: he represented the other face of the eighteenth century. The hymn was his element, indeed he was the hymn: examining his writings, we have the sensation of finding ourselves in the presence of an initiate to whom great secrets were transmitted and who, exceptionally, did not waste his ingenuity upon them. A true mystic, he disliked irony — antireligious by definition, irony never pays; how could this man who had cast the world behind him have resorted to it, who perhaps knew but one pride, that of the Sigh? "All nature is but a concentrated suffering"; "If I had not found God, my mind could never have attached itself to anything on earth"; "I had the happiness to feel and to say that I would believe myself wretched indeed if something prospered for me in the world." And let us add this vast metaphysical disappointment: "Solomon reports having seen everything under the sun. I could cite someone who would not be lying if he said he had seen something more: that is, everything above the sun; and that someone is very far from glorying in what he has seen."

As discreet as they are profound, such notations (taken chiefly from the posthumously published works) cannot win us over to the intolerable lyricism of *L'Homme de Désir,* where everything is vexing except the title, and where, unfortunately for the reader, Rousseau is present on every page. A curious fate, let us remark in passing, that of Rousseau, acting on others only by his dubious aspects, and whose windiness and jargon have spoiled the style of a Saint-Martin as much as that of a . . . Robespierre. The declamatory tone before, during, and after the Revolution, everything that heralds, reveals, and disqualifies Romanticism, the horrors of poetic prose in general, stem from this paradoxically inspired and unsound mind, responsible for the generalization of bad taste toward the end of the eighteenth century and the beginning of the next. A deadly influence that marked Chateaubriand and Senancour, and that only Joubert managed to escape. Saint-Martin yielded to it all the more readily because his literary instincts were never very certain. As for his ideas, pastured in the vague, they were capable of exasperating Voltaire, who after reading the book *Des Erreurs et de la Vérité* wrote to d'Alembert, "I do not believe that anything more absurd, more obscure, more insane, and more foolish has ever been printed." It is irritating that de Maistre should have shown a pronounced taste for this work, though this appeared, it is true, at a time when he was sacrificing both to Rousseauism and to theosophy. But at the very moment he was renouncing one and the other, moving away from illuminism and, in a spasm of ingratitude and ill humor, taxing Freemasonry with "stupidity," he kept all his sympathy for the *philosophe inconnu* whose theses on "primitive knowledge," matter, sacrifice, and salvation by blood he had adopted and developed. Would the very notion of the Fall have assumed such importance for him had it not been vigorously affirmed by Saint-Martin? The notion was certainly banal, even stale, but in rejuvenating it, rethinking it as a free mind disengaged from all orthodoxy, our theosophist conferred upon it that extra authority which only the heterodox can impart to tired religious themes. He did the same for the notion of Providence, which, preached (thanks to him) in the Lodges of the period, acquired a seductiveness it could have received from no Church. It was also one of Saint-Martin's merits to have given — in the midst of "endless progress" — a religious accent to the malaise of living in time, to the horror of being imprisoned within it. De Maistre would follow him on this path, though with less exaltation and ardor. Time, he tells us, is "something compelled that asks only to end"; "Man is subject to time, and nonetheless he is by nature alien to time, so much so that the notion of eternal happiness, joined to that of time, fatigues and frightens him."

In de Maistre's thought, entrance into eternity is effected not by ecstasy, by the individual leap into the absolute, but by the mediation of an extraordinary event, one likely to seal off becoming — and not by the instantaneous suppression of time achieved in delight, but by the end of time, the denouement of the historical process in its entirety. It is — need we repeat? — as a prophet and not as a mystic that de Maistre envisages our relations with the temporal universe: "There is no longer any religion on earth: the human race cannot remain in this state. Dreadful oracles announce, moreover, that 'the time has come.' "

Each epoch tends to think that it is in some sense the last, that with it ends a cycle or all cycles. Today as yesterday, we conceive hell more readily than the golden age, apocalypse than utopia, and the idea of a cosmic catastrophe is as familiar to us as it was to the Buddhists, to the pre-Socratics, or to the Stoics. The vivacity of our terrors keeps us in an unstable equilibrium, favorable to the flowering of the prophetic gift. This is singularly true for the periods following great convulsions. The passion for prophesying then seizes everyone; skeptics and fanatics alike delight in the idea of disaster and give themselves up in concert to the pleasure of having foreseen and trumpeted it abroad. But it is especially the theoreticians of Reaction who exult (tragically, no doubt) over the reality or the imminence of the worst — of the worst that is their raison d'être. "I am dying with Europe," de Maistre wrote in 1819. Two years earlier, in a letter to de Maistre himself, Bonald had expressed an analogous certitude: "I have no news for you; you are in a position to judge what we are and where we are going. Moreover, for me there are certain things that are absolutely inexplicable, escape from which does not seem to me within human power, insofar as men act by their own lights and under the influence of their wills alone; and in truth, what I see most clearly in all this . . . is the Apocalypse."

After conceiving the Restoration, both men were disappointed to see that once it had become a reality, it failed to erase the vestiges of the Revolution in men's minds —

a disappointment that they anticipated, perhaps, judging from the eagerness with which they abandoned themselves to it. Whatever the case, the course they assigned to history was quite ignored by history itself: it flouted their projects, it belied their systems. De Maistre's darkest observations, the ones that reveal a "romantic" complacency, date from the period when his ideas seem to have triumphed. In a letter of September 6, 1817, he writes to his daughter Constance, ". . . an invisible iron arm has always been over me, like a dreadful nightmare that keeps me from running, even from breathing."

The rebuffs he suffered from King Victor-Emmanuel doubtless had much to do with these fits of depression, but what disturbed him most was the prospect of new upheavals, the specter of democracy. Unwilling to resign himself to the future forming before his eyes, though he had foreseen it, he hoped — with the incurable optimism of the defeated — that since his ideal was threatened, everything else was, too; that along with the form of civilization he approved of, civilization itself was disappearing: an illusion as frequent as it is inevitable. How to dissociate oneself from a historical reality that is collapsing, especially when it was previously in accord with one's inmost self? Finding it impossible to endorse the future, one lets oneself be tempted by the notion of decadence, which, without being true or false, at least explains why each period, in attempting to achieve its own individuality, does so only by sacrificing certain very real and irreplaceable earlier values.

The old regime had to perish: a principle of exhaustion had undermined it long before the Revolution came to finish it off. Should we deduce from this the superiority of the Third Estate? Not at all, for the bourgeoisie, despite its virtues and its reserves of vitality, by the quality of its tastes marked no "progress" over the fallen nobility. The relays occurring down through history reveal the urgency less than the automatism of change. If in the absolute nothing is dated, in the relative, in the immediate, everything risks being so, for the new constitutes the sole criterion, metamorphosis the sole morality. To grasp the meaning of events, let us envisage them as a substance offered to the eye of an utterly disabused observer. The makers of history do not understand it, and those who participate in it to any extent are its dupes or its accomplices. Only the degree of our disillusion guarantees the objectivity of our judgments, but "life" being partiality, error, illusion, and will-to-illusion, is not the passing of objective judgments a passage to the realm of death?

The Third Estate, in asserting itself, would necessarily be impermeable to elegance, to refinement, to a worthy skepticism, to the manners and the style that defined the old regime. All progress implies a retreat, any rise a fall; but if we collapse as we advance, that collapse is limited to a circumscribed sector. The advent of the bourgeoisie liberated the energies it had accumulated during its forced absence from political life; from this perspective, the change provoked by the Revolution incontestably represents a step forward. The same is true of the appearance on the political stage of the proletariat, destined in its turn to replace a sterile and ankylosed class; but it is just here that a principle of retrogradation functions, since the last-comers cannot safeguard certain values that redeem the vices of the liberal era: the horror of uniformity, the sense of adventure and of risk, the passion for a relaxed tone in intellectual matters, the imperialist appetite on the level of the individual, much more than on that of the collectivity. . . .

An inexorable law strikes and directs societies and civilizations. When, for lack of vitality, the past collapses, clinging to it serves no purpose — and yet it is this attachment to antiquated forms of life, to lost or bad causes, that makes so touching the anathemas of a de Maistre or a Bonald. Everything seems admirable and everything is false in the utopian vision; everything is execrable and everything seems true in the observations of the reactionaries.

It goes without saying that in positing heretofore so clear-cut a distinction between Revolution and Reaction, we have necessarily sacrificed to naïveté or to laziness, to the comfort of definitions. One always simplifies out of facility — whence the attraction of the abstract. The concrete, fortunately exposing the convenience of our explanations and our concepts, teaches us that a revolution that has run its course, that has established itself, becomes the contrary of a fermentation and a birth, ceases to be a revolution, that it imitates and must imitate the features, the apparatus, and even the functioning of the order it has overturned; the more it exerts itself in doing so (and it cannot do otherwise), the more it will destroy its principles and its prestige. Henceforth conservative in its way, it will do battle to defend not the past but the present. Here nothing will help it so as much as following the paths and the methods employed by the regime it has abolished. Hence, in order to insure the permanence of the conquests it prides itself on, the revolution will turn from the exalted visions and dreams from which it had formerly drawn the elements of its dynamism. Only the prerevolutionary condition is truly revolutionary, the one in which men's minds subscribe to the double cult of the future and of destruction. So long as a revolution is only a possibility, it transcends history's givens and constants; it exceeds, so to speak, its context. But once it has occurred, it conforms to that context and, prolonging the past, follows its ruts — all the more successfully if it utilizes the techniques of the reaction it had previously condemned. Every anarchist conceals, in the depth of his rebellions, a reactionary who is awaiting his hour, the hour of taking power, when the metamorphosis of chaos into . . . authority raises problems no utopia dares solve or even contemplate without falling into lyricism or absurdity.

Every impulse of renovation, at the very moment when it approaches its goal, when it realizes itself through the State, creeps toward the automatism of the old institutions and assumes the face of tradition. As it defines and confirms itself, it loses energy, and this is also true of ideas: the more formulated and explicit they are, the more their efficacy diminishes. A distinct idea is an idea without a future. Beyond their virtual status, thought and action degrade and annul themselves: one ends up as system, the other as power: two forms of sterility and failure. Though we can endlessly debate the destiny of revolutions, political or otherwise, a single feature is common to them all, a single certainty: the disappointment they generate in all who have believed in them with some fervor.

That the basic, essential renewal of human realities is conceivable in itself but unrealizable in fact should make us more understanding with regard to a de Maistre. Though we may regard one or another of his opinions as abhorrent, he is nonetheless the representative of that philosophy immanent to any regime congealed in terror and dogmas. Where can we find a theoretician more fanatically opposed to becoming, to praxis? He hated action as the prefiguration of a rupture, as the likelihood of becoming, since for him to act was to remake. The revolutionary himself deals this way with the present in which he installs himself and which he would eternalize; but his present will soon be the past, and by clinging to it he ends up joining the advocates of tradition.

The tragic aspect of the political universe resides in that hidden force which leads every movement to deny itself, to betray its original inspiration, and to corrupt itself as it confirms itself, as it advances. This is because in politics, as in everything, we fulfill ourselves only upon our own ruins. Revolutions start in order to give a meaning to history; such meaning has already been given, replies reaction, we must submit to it and defend it. This is exactly what will be maintained by a revolution that has triumphed; hence intolerance results from a hypothesis that has degenerated into a certitude and that is imposed as such by a regime — from a vision promoted to the rank of truth. Each doctrine contains, in germ, infinite possibilities for disaster: since the mind is constructive only by inadvertence, the encounter of man and idea almost always involves a deadly sequel.

Imbued with the futility of reforms, with the vanity and the heresy of improvements, reactionaries would spare humanity the lacerations and exhaustions of hope, the pangs of an illusory quest: be satisfied with what has already

been acquired, they suggest; abdicate your anxieties in order to bask in the bliss of stagnation and, opting for an
irrevocably official state of affairs, choose finally between
the instinct for preservation and the craving for tragedy.
But man, open to all choices, rejects precisely this one. In
this rejection, in this impossibility, his drama is played
out, whence it comes about that he is at once, or alternately, a reactionary and a revolutionary animal. Fragile
though the classical distinction may be, moreover, between the concept of revolution and that of reaction, we
must nonetheless retain it, on pain of chaos or confusion
in the consideration of political phenomena. It constitutes
a reference point as problematical as it is indispensable, a
suspect but inevitable and obligatory convention. And it
is also the one that obliges us constantly to speak of
"right" and "left," terms that have no correspondence to
intrinsic and irreducible givens, terms so summary that we
should like to leave to demagogues alone the faculty and
the pleasure of utilizing them. It sometimes happens that
the right (we need merely think of national uprisings) prevails over the left in vigor, force, and dynamism; espousing the characteristics of revolutionary spirit, it then ceases
to be the expression of an ossified world, of a group of
interests or of a declining class. Conversely, the left,
snagged in the mechanism of power or imprisoned by antiquated superstitions, can easily lose its virtues, harden,
and exhibit the very flaws that commonly affect the right.
Vitality being no one's privilege, the analyst must determine its presence and intensity with no concern for the
doctrinal varnish of this or that movement, this or that
political or social reality. Next let us consider nations:
some make their revolution on the right, others on the left.
Though the former's revolution is often but a simulacrum,
it nonetheless exists, and this alone reveals the inanity of

any univocal determination of the notion of revolution. "Right" and "left": simple approximations that unfortunately we cannot do without. Not to resort to them would be to renounce taking sides, to suspend one's judgment in political matters, to free oneself of the servitudes of duration, to require of man that he waken to the absolute, that he become uniquely a metaphysical animal. Such an effort of emancipation, such a leap outside our sleepers' truths, is accessible to few. We are all dozing, and paradoxically, that is why we take action. Let us continue, then, as if nothing had occurred, let us go on making our traditional distinctions, happy not to know that the values appearing in time are, in the last instance, interchangeable.

The reasons that impel the political world to forge its concepts and categories are quite different from those invoked by a theoretical discipline; if they appear equally necessary to both, those of the former still conceal realities that are less honorable: all doctrines of action and of combat, with their apparatus and their schemas, were invented only to give men a good conscience, permitting them to hate each other . . . nobly, without embarrassment, without remorse. Upon reflection, would it not be legitimate to conclude that when facing events, the free mind, refractory to the play of ideologies but still subject to time, has a choice only between despair and opportunism?

De Maistre could no more be an opportunist than he could despair: his religion, his principles, forbade it. But with his moods prevailing over his faith, he frequently had fits of discouragement, especially at the spectacle of a civilization without a future: witness his observations on Europe. He was not the only man who believed that he was dying with the continent. . . . In the last century and in ours, many have been convinced that Europe was on the point of expiring, or that it had only one recourse: to conceal its decrepitude by means of coquetry. The notion that the continent was in its death agony had spread and acquired a certain vogue on the occasion of the great defeats — in France after 1814, 1870, and 1940; in Germany after the collapse of 1918, or that of 1945. Yet Europe, indifferent to its Cassandras, cheerfully perseveres in its agony, and that agony, so stubborn, so durable, is perhaps equivalent to a new life. This whole problem — which comes down to a question of perspective and of ideology — if it is meaningless for Marxists, nonetheless preoccupies both liberals and conservatives, horrified as they are (though as defenders of different positions) to be witnessing the disappearance of their reasons for living, of their doctrines, and of their superstitions. That a form of Europe is dying today, no one will dispute, though such a death must be seen as no more than a simple stage of an immense decline. With Bergson died, according to Valéry, "the last representative of European intelligence." The formula might serve for other homages or speeches, for we shall find for a long while to come some "last representative" of the Western mind. . . . He who proclaims the end of "civilization" or of "intelligence" does so out of rancor toward a future that to him seems hostile, and out of vengeance against history, faithless history that does not deign to conform to his image of it. De Maistre was dying with his own Europe, with the Europe that rejected the spirit of innovation — "the greatest scourge," as he called it. It was his conviction that in order to save societies from disorder, a universal idea, acknowledged by fair means or foul, was necessary, which would eliminate the danger of entertaining, in religion and in politics, novelty, approximation, theoretical scruples. That this universal idea was incarnated in Catholicism he had no doubt, the diversity of regimes, of mores, and of gods troubling him not at all. Against the relativism of experience he set up the absolute of dogma; that a religion might cease to submit to it, that it might permit private judgment and liberty of thought, he declared harmful and did not hesitate to deny in the name of religion. "Mohammedanism and paganism itself would have done less harm politically if they had been substituted for Christianity, with their species of dogmas and faith; for they are religions, and Protestantism is no such thing." So long as he maintained some loyalty to the principles of Freemasonry, he remained quite open to a certain liberalism; once his hatred of the Revolution drove him into the arms of the Church, he slid toward intolerance.

Whether they take their inspiration from utopia or from reaction, absolutisms resemble and unite with each other. Independent of their doctrinal content, which differentiates them only on the surface, they participate in one and the same schema, one and the same logical process, a phenomenon proper to all the systems that, not content to posit an unconditional principle, also make of it a dogma and a law. An identical mode of thought presides over the elaboration of theories that are materially dissimilar but formally analogous. As for the doctrines of Unity, they are so closely related that to study one, whatever it may be, is thereby to scrutinize all the regimes that, rejecting diversity in concept and in practice, deny man the right to heresy, to singularity, or to doubt.

Obsessed with Unity, de Maistre raves against any attempt likely to dissolve it, against the least impulse of innovation or even of autonomy, without realizing that heresy represents the sole possibility of reinvigorating men's consciences, that by shaking them up it preserves them from the sluggishness into which conformism plunges them, and that if heresy weakens the Church, on the other hand it reinforces religion. Any official god is a god alone, abandoned, soured. We pray with fervor only in sects, among persecuted minorities, in darkness and in fear, conditions indispensable to the proper exercise of piety. But for a de Maistre, submission — I should say, rather, the rage of submission — surpasses the effusions of faith. Lutherans, Calvinists, Jansenists were, if we are to believe him, merely rebels, conspirators, traitors; he abhors them and advises, for their annihilation, the use of all means that are not "crimes." Yet if we read his apology for the Inquisition, our impression is that even this last resort is one he does not entirely reject. De Maistre is the Machiavelli of theocracy.

Unity, as he conceives of it, presents itself in a double aspect: metaphysical and historical. On the one hand, it signifies triumph over division, evil, and sin; on the other, definitive instauration, final apotheosis of Catholicism through the victory over temptations and modern errors. Unity on the level of eternity; unity on the level of time. If the first transcends us, if it escapes our possibilities for control, the second we can envisage and deal with. Let us say it straight off: it seems to us illusory; it leaves us skeptical. For we do not see what religious idea would today be capable of achieving the spiritual and political unification of the world. Christianity is too weak to seduce or to subdue men's minds; an ideology or a conqueror must be resorted to. Will the task fall to Marxism, or to a Caesarism of a new type? Or to both at once? Such a synthesis seems dismaying only to reason, but not to history, that reign of anomaly.

That Catholicism, better still that the Christian religion in its entirety, should be in utter deliquescence, our experience teaches us every day: as it now appears — prudent, accommodating, measured — Christianity would not tolerate an apologist so fierce, so magnificently unbridled, as de Maistre, who would not have denounced with such fury "the sectarian spirit" in others had he not been uniquely imbued with it himself. The man who cursed the Terror does not find one word with which to castigate the Revocation of the Edict of Nantes; he even applauds it: "With regard to the manufactures taken by the refugees into foreign countries, and to the wrong done to France as a result, the persons for whom these shopkeeping objections signify something . . ." Shopkeeping objections! Unsurpassable, his bad faith is either a joke or a sort of madness: "Louis XIV crushed Protestantism and died in his bed, covered with glory and heavy with years; Louis XVI toyed with the thing and died on the scaffold."

In another place, in a fit of . . . moderation, de Maistre acknowledges that the critical spirit, a spirit of protest, appears well before Luther, and he rightly traces it back to Celsus, to the very beginnings of the opposition to Christianity. For the Roman patrician, in effect, the Christian was a dismaying, actually inconceivable phenomenon, a subject of stupor. In his *True Discourse,* a moving text if ever there was one, Celsus raves against the actions of this new sect that has managed, through its intrigues and its excesses, to aggravate the situation of the empire, presently beleaguered by the Barbarians. He did not understand why a man might prefer to Greek philosophy a suspect and nebulous teaching which disgusted him but of which, not without a certain despair, he foresaw the contagious power and the terrible opportunities. Sixteen centuries later, his argumentation and his invective were adopted by Voltaire, who, similarly aghast at Christianity's amazing career, did his best to advertise its ravages and its abuses. That such a work, whose salubrity leaps to the eye, should be at the origin of the Terror is another exaggeration of de Maistre's, for whom *irreligion* and *scaffold* are correlative terms. "We must absolutely slay the spirit of the eighteenth century," he urges, forgetting that this spirit he so hates had only one fanaticism, that of tolerance. And then by what right condemn the guillotine when one has been so tender about the stake? The contradiction does not seem to disturb the admirer of the Inquisition; servant of one cause, he legitimated its excesses while execrating those committed in the name of another. This is the paradox of the partisan mind, and it is an eternal one.

To regard the eighteenth century as the privileged moment, as the very incarnation of evil, is to indulge in aberrations. In what other period were injustices denounced so rigorously? A salutary oeuvre of which the Terror was the negation and not the consummation.

"Never," says Tocqueville, "had tolerance in religion, mildness in command, humanity, and even benevolence been more extolled and, it appeared, more acknowledged than in the eighteenth century; the right to wage war, which is in a sense the last refuge of violence, was itself confined and rationalized. Yet from the heart of such gentle manners would nonetheless emerge the most inhuman revolution."

In reality, the period, too "civilized," had achieved a refinement that doomed it to fragility, to a brilliant and ephemeral term. "Gentle manners" and dissolute ones go together, as is proved by the Regency, the most agreeable and most lucid — hence the most corrupt — era of modern history. The vertigo of being free was beginning to weigh on men's minds. Already Madame du Deffand, more indicative of the century than Voltaire himself, had remarked that liberty was "not a good thing for everyone," that rare were those who could tolerate its "darkness and its emptiness." And it was to flee this "emptiness" and this "darkness," it seems to us, that France flung herself into the wars of the Revolution and of the Empire, in which she willingly sacrificed those habits of independence, of defiance, and of analysis that a hundred years of conversation and skepticism had enabled her to acquire. Threatened with disaggregation by this debauch of irony and intelligence, France would recover her balance through the collective adventure, through a craving for submission on a national scale. "Men," de Maistre informs us, "can never be united for any goal whatever without a law or a rule that deprives them of their will: one must be a priest or a soldier."

This vice of our nature, far from saddening de Maistre, delights him, and he seizes upon it in order to praise to the skies the papacy, royalty, the Spanish tribunals, and all the symbols of authority. Of the Jesuits, those accomplices of autocracies, he was first the pupil, later the spokesman; and such were his admiration and his gratitude that he admits to being indebted to them "for not having been an orator of the Constituent Assembly." The judgments he passes on himself almost always concern the Revolution and his relations with it; and it is always with regard to the Revolution that he defends or denigrates France. This Savoyard who once called himself "the most French of all foreigners" is one of those who best penetrated the genius of the "initiator nation," destined — by its dominant quality, the spirit of proselytism — to exercise over Europe a "veritable magistracy." Providence having decreed, he tells us, "the era of the French," he cites in their regard Isaiah's phrase: "Every word of this people is a conspiracy." Applied to France at that moment, the phrase was true; it would be less so subsequently, and would cease to have any meaning at all after the war of 1914.

If the Revolution was present in all the shocks of the nineteenth century, none of them could equal it. Obsessed by the figures of '89, the insurgents of 48, paralyzed by the fear of betraying their models, were epigones, prisoners of a style of revolt that they had not created and that was, so to speak, imposed upon them. A nation never produces two great revolutionary ideas, nor two radically different forms of messianism. It gives its measure but once, in a circumscribed, defined epoch, the supreme moment of its expansion, when it triumphs with all its truths and all its lies; it exhausts itself afterward, as does the mission with which it was invested.

Since the October Revolution, Russia has exerted the same kind of influence, terror, and fascination that France generated in 1789. In its turn, Russia has imposed its ideas on a world that welcomes them, subjugated, trembling, or zealous. And its proselytizing power is even greater than France's was; de Maistre, today, would maintain more appropriately that Providence had, this time, decreed "the era of the Russians"; he would even apply to them Isaiah's phrase, and perhaps would also say of them that they are an "initiator nation." Moreover, in the very period he lived among them, he was far from underestimating their capacities: "There is no man who desires as passionately as the Russian"; "if we could imprison a Russian desire beneath a fortress, that fortress would explode." The nation that at the time was said to be indolent and apathetic to him seemed "the most mobile, the most impetuous, the most enterprising in the universe." The world did not begin to realize as much until after the Decembrist rebellion (1825), a crucial event after which reactionaries and liberals — the former out of apprehension, the latter out of desire — began predicting upheavals in Russia: here was evidence of the future that required, in order to be proclaimed, no prophetic faculty. Never had anyone seen a revolution so sure to come, so expected, as the Russian Revolution: the most widespread reforms, the humanization of the regime, the best will in the world, the largest concessions — nothing could have stopped it. There was no merit in its explosion, since it existed, so to speak, before appearing and since it could be described down to the last detail (one need merely think of *The Possessed*) before manifesting itself.

Since the only guarantors of "good order" were, in de Maistre's eyes, slavery and religion, he advocated the maintenance of serfdom for the consolidation of czarist power, since the Orthodox Church he disdained seemed to him adulterated, warped, contaminated by Protestantism, and, in any case, unlikely to counterbalance subversive ideas. But did the Catholic Church, in the name of the true religion, succeed in preventing the Revolution in France? He never even asks himself the question; what interests de Maistre is absolute government, and in his opinion all government is absolute government, for, he claims, "the moment it can be resisted on the pretext of error or injustice, it no longer exists."

That occasionally one encounters in de Maistre impulses of liberalism — echoes of his early education or expressions of a more or less conscious remorse — is undeniable. Yet the "human" side of his doctrines is of only mediocre interest. Since his talents ripen and really function only in his antimodern excesses, his outrages to common sense, it is natural that it should be the reactionary in him who holds our attention. Every time he insults our principles or upbraids our superstitions in the name of his own, we have occasion to rejoice: the writer then excels and outdoes himself. The darker his vision, the more he will enfold it in a light, transparent appearance. The impulsive aesthete that he was concerned himself, even in the midst of his high rages, with the minuscule problems of language; he fulminated as a litterateur, even as a grammarian, and his frenzies not only failed to diminish his passion for the correct and elegant formulation but augmented it even more. An epileptic temperament infatuated with the trifles of the Word: trances and boutades, convulsions and bagatelles, grace and a foaming mouth — everything combined to compose that pamphleteering universe at whose heart he harried "error" with blows of invective, those ultimatums of impotence. It was his humiliation that he could never erect his prejudices and his fixations into laws. He took revenge for this situation through utterance, whose virulence sustained in him the illusion of efficacy. Never seeking a truth for its own sake but only in order to make it an instrument of combat, unable to acknowledge others' absolutes (or to be indifferent to them), defining himself by his refusals and still more by his aversions, de Maistre needed, for the exercise of his intelligence, inveterately to execrate someone or something, and to brood over his or its suppression. This was an imperative, a condition indispensable to the fecundity of his disequilibrium, without which he would have fallen into sterility, the curse of thinkers who refuse to cultivate their disagreements with others or with themselves. The spirit of tolerance, had he yielded to it, would not have failed to smother his genius. We may further note that for someone so sincerely taken with paradox, the one way of being original, after a whole century of declamations concerning liberty and justice, was to embrace the opposing opinions, to hurl himself upon other fictions, upon those of authority — in short, to exchange aberrations.

When, in 1797, Napoleon read in Milan the *Considérations sur la France,* perhaps he saw in them a justification of his own ambitions and something like the itinerary of his own dreams: he had only to interpret to his advantage the arguments for royalty that de Maistre made there. On the other hand, the speeches and writings of the liberals (of Necker, of Madame de Staël, and of Benjamin Constant) must have vexed him, since he found in them, according to the expression of Albert Sorel, "the theory of the obstacles to his reign." Repudiating the concept of destiny, liberal thought could scarcely beguile a conqueror who, not content to meditate upon destiny, still

aspired to incarnate it, to be its concrete image, its histor-
ical translation, tending as he did by nature to rely on
Providence and to consider himself its interpreter. The
Considérations revealed Bonaparte to himself.

Too much is made of love-hate, and we forget that
there exists an even murkier and more complex sentiment:
admiration-hate, the very feeling that de Maistre nourished for Napoleon. How lucky to have for one's contemporary a tyrant worthy of being abhorred, to whom one
might dedicate a cult in reverse and whom, secretly, one
would like to resemble! In obliging his enemies to raise
themselves to his level, compelling them to jealousy,
Napoleon was a real blessing. Without him neither
Chateaubriand nor Constant nor de Maistre could so
readily have resisted the temptation to measure, to proportion: the histrionics of the first, the instability of the
second, and the rages of the third partook of his own histrionics, his instability, his rages. The horror he inspired
in them included a good deal of fascination. To combat a
"monster" is necessarily to possess some mysterious affinities with him, and also to borrow from him certain character traits. De Maistre recalls Luther, whom he insulted
so, and even more Voltaire, the man he attacked most, as
well as the Pascal of the *Provincial Letters,* enemy of the
Jesuits — that is, the Pascal whom he loathed. As a good
pamphleteer, he set upon the pamphleteers of the other
side, whom he understood so well, for like them he had a
mania for inexactitude and a talent for parti pris. When
he defines philosophy as the art of disdaining objections,
he defines his own method, his own "art." Yet preposter-
ous as it seems, the assertion is nonetheless true, or almost
true: who would defend a position, who would support
an idea, if he had to multiply his scruples, ceaselessly

weigh pros and cons, and conduct a reasoning with all due precautions? The original thinker forges ahead rather than digging in: he is a *Draufgänger,* an enthusiast, a break-neck, and in any case a determined, combative mind, a rebel in the realm of abstraction, whose aggressiveness, though sometimes veiled, is nonetheless real and effective. Under his apparently neutral preoccupations, camouflaged as problems, stirs a will, functions an instinct, as indispensable as intelligence to the creation of a system: without the collaboration of that instinct and that will, how to triumph over objections and over the paralysis to which they doom the mind? No assertion that cannot be annihilated by a contrary assertion. In order to offer any opinion about anything, bravura action and a certain capacity for thoughtlessness are necessary, as well as a propensity for letting oneself be carried away by extrarational reasons. "The entire human race," de Maistre says, "is descended from one couple. This truth has been denied like all the rest; and what of that?" This means of disposing of objections is practiced by anyone who identifies himself with a doctrine or who merely adopts a well-defined viewpoint on any subject; but rare are those who dare acknowledge as much, who have probity enough to divulge the method they employ and must employ, on pain of hardening into approximation or silence. In one of those blunders that do him honor, de Maistre, priding himself on an abusive use of "and what of that?," implicitly yields the secret of his extravagances.

Not at all exempt from that naïveté so characteristic of dogmatism, he will make himself the interpreter of all the possessors of a certitude and will proclaim his happiness and theirs: "We, happy possessors of the truth" — a triumphal language that for the rest of us remains inconceivable but that delights and fortifies the believer. A faith that acknowledges other faiths, that does not believe itself to possess a monopoly on truth, is doomed to ruin, abandoning the absolute that legitimates it, resigning itself to being no more than a phenomenon of civilization, an episode, an accident. A religion's degree of inhumanity guarantees its strength and its duration: a liberal religion is a mockery or a miracle. Reality, a terrible and exact observation, true at every point for the Judeo-Christian world; to posit a single god is to profess intolerance and to subscribe, willy-nilly, to the theocratic ideal. On a more general level, the doctrines of Unity proceed from the same spirit: even when they lay claim to antireligious ideas, they follow the formal schema of theocracy, they even boil down to a secularized theocracy. Positivism derived a great advantage from "retrograde" systems, whose content and beliefs it rejected only to adopt their logical armature, their abstract contours. Auguste Comte treated de Maistre's ideas as Marx treated Hegel's.

Variously curious as to the fate of religion but equally subjugated by their respective systems, positivists and Catholics exploited to the best of their abilities the thought of the author of *Du Pape;* freer, Baudelaire found in it, out of sheer inner necessity, several themes, such as those of evil and of sin, or certain of his "prejudices" against democratic ideas and "progress." When Baudelaire makes "true civilization" consist in the "diminution of the traces of original sin," is he not inspired by that passage of the *Soirées* where the perfect "state of civilization" is presented as a reality situated outside the realm of the Fall? "De Maistre and Edgar Poe have taught me to reason": perhaps it would have been more precise on Baudelaire's part to admit that the ultramontanist thinker had furnished him with obsessions. When he invokes a "diabolic providence" or professes "satanism," Baudelaire turns certain Maistrian motifs inside out, aggravating them and lending them a character of concrete negativity. The philosophy of the Restoration had certain rather unexpected literary extensions: the influence of Bonald on Balzac was as powerful as that of de Maistre on Baudelaire. Probe the past of a writer (especially of a poet), examine in detail the elements of his intellectual biography, and you will always find some reactionary antecedents. . . . Memory is the condition of poetry, the past its substance. And what does Reaction assert, if not the supreme value of the past?

"What one believes true, one must say, and say it boldly; I should like, were it to cost me dear, to discover a truth likely to shock the entire human race: I should tell it point-blank." The Baudelaire of "absolute frankness," of *Fusées* and of *Mon Coeur mis à nu*, is contained and somehow heralded in this remark from the *Soirées*, which gives us the recipe for that incomparable art of provocation in which Baudelaire was to distinguish himself almost as much as de Maistre. Everyone distinguishes himself there, moreover, who — whether with lucidity or with acrimony — rejects the clever enchantments of Progress. Why do conservatives wield invective so well, and for the most part write more carefully than the adepts of the future? It is because, furious at being contradicted by events, they fling themselves, in their confusion, upon the Word, from which, lacking a more substantial resource, they derive vengeance and consolation. The others resort to it more casually and even with contempt: accomplices of the future, sure of themselves with regard to "history," they write without art, even without passion, conscious as they are that style is the prerogative and somehow the luxury of failure. When we speak of failure, we are thinking not only of de Maistre but also of Saint-Simon. In one as in the other, the same exclusive, limited attachment to the cause of the aristocracy, a host of prejudices defended with a continual rage, the pride of caste carried to ostentation, and a similar incapacity to act, which explains why they were so enterprising as writers. When the former concerns himself with problems, when the latter describes events, the slightest idea, the merest fact, explodes under the passion each invests in it. Trying to dissect their prose is tantamount to analyzing a thunderstorm. Far be it from us, however, to put the duke and the count on the same footing: the former restored and recreated an epoch, he worked straight from life, whereas the latter was content to animate ideas; now, with concepts, how attain to the plenitude of genius? There is no true creation in philosophy: whatever depth and originality it achieves, thought always maintains itself at a derived level, this side of Being's movement and activity; art alone rises to that height, art alone imitates God or substitutes for Him. The thinker exhausts the definition of the incomplete man.

Saint-Simon, according to Sainte-Beuve, suggests a mélange of Shakespeare and Tacitus; for us, de Maistre would evoke — a less felicitous mixture — Cardinal Bellarmine and Voltaire, a theologian and a litterateur. If we cite the name of the great controversialist, that professional of quibbling who raged against Protestantism in the sixteenth century, it is because de Maistre, with more verve and more spirit, was to wage the same campaign: was he not, in some sense, the last representative of the Counter-Reformation?

Contemplating his transports against the new "sects," we sometimes wonder if there is not a degree of humor in all this deployment of rage: is it conceivable that in writing certain diatribes, de Maistre was not conscious of the enormities he was uttering? And yet (we can never say it often enough) it is these enormities that rescue his works and lure us to read them still. When, on the subject of an assertion of Bacon's, he exclaims, "No, never since *Fiat Lux* was spoken has the human ear heard anything equal," such extravagance delights us, as does this: "The priests have preserved everything, have revived everything, and have taught us everything." An insane assertion, whose savor is undeniable: in making it, did the author become the accomplice of our smiles? And when he assures us that the Pope is the "demiurge of civilization," does he intend to divert us, or is this what he truly thinks? It would be simplest to admit that he was sincere; moreover, we discern not the slightest trace of charlatanism in his life: lucidity, in his case, never went to the lengths of imposture or farce. . . . That is the sole failing in his sense of excess.

There was in this conservative who destroyed in the name of tradition, in this fanatic by discipline and by method, a desire to possess unshakable convictions, a need to be all of a piece. "I fall into an idea as from a precipice," complained a sick man; de Maistre could have said as much, though with this difference, that he *longed* to fall there, that he burned to be engulfed, and that like certain aggressive thinkers, enraged thinkers, he was impatient to take us down with him — abyssal proselytism that is the mark of fanaticism, innate or acquired. His, though acquired, the result of effort and deliberation, he assimilated perfectly, and made it his organic reality. Nailed to the absolute out of hatred of a century that had called everything into question, he would go too far in the other direction and, out of fear or doubt, would erect deliberate blindness into a system. Never to be short of illusions, to obnubilate himself: such was his dream. He had the good fortune to realize it.

Despite his moments of clairvoyance, he was nonetheless mistaken in many of his expectations. The mission of France, he imagined, was the religious regeneration of humanity. France turned to secularity. . . . He predicted the end of schisms, the return of the separated churches to Catholicism, the reconquest by the Sovereign Pontiff of his ancient privileges. Rome, abandoned to herself, is more modest, more timid, than ever. If he foresaw some of the convulsions that were to shake Europe, he did not divine those to which we are prey. But the nullity of his prophecies should not make us lose sight of the merits or the actuality of this theoretician of order and authority who, had he had the luck to be better known, would have been the inspiration of every form of political orthodoxy, the genius and the providence of all our century's despotisms. His thought is incontestably alive today, but only to the degree that it repels or disconcerts: the more we frequent him, the more we are reminded, a contrario, of the delights of skepticism or of the crying need for a vindication of heresy.

1957

3

Fractures

✳

WHEN ONE HAS EMERGED from the circle of errors and illusions within which actions are performed, taking a position is virtually an impossibility. A minimum of silliness is essential for everything, for affirming and even for denying.

✳

To glimpse the essential, no need to ply a trade. Stay flat on your back all day long, and moan. . . .

✳

Whatever puts me at odds with the world is consubstantial with myself. How little I have learned from experience. My disappointments have always preceded me.

✳

There exists an undeniable pleasure in knowing that everything you do has no real basis, that whether or not you commit an action is a matter of indifference. The fact nonetheless remains that in our daily gestures we compromise with Vacuity — that is, we turn and turn about, and occasionally, at the same time, we take the world as real and unreal. We mingle pure truths and sordid truths and this amalgam, the thinker's disgrace, is the living man's revenge.

*

It is not the violent evils that mark us but the secret, insistent, tolerable ones belonging to our daily round and undermining us as conscientiously as Time itself.

*

After a quarter of an hour, no one can observe another's despair without impatience.

*

Friendship has scope and interest only for the young. For an older person, it is apparent that what he dreads most is being survived by his friends.

*

One can imagine everything, predict everything, save how low one can sink.

*

What still attaches me to things is a thirst inherited from ancestors who carried the curiosity to exist to the point of ignominy.

*

How we must have loathed each other in the pestilential darkness of the caves! Easy to understand why the painters who managed to keep body and soul together there had no desire to immortalize the image of their kind — why they preferred the figures of animals.

*

"Having renounced sanctity . . .": to think I could have uttered such a thing! I must have an excuse, and I don't despair of finding it.

*

Except for music, everything is a lie, even solitude, even ecstasy. Music, in fact, is the one and the other, *only better*.

*

How age simplifies everything! At the library I ask for four books. Two are set in type that is too small; I discard them without even considering their contents. The third, too . . . serious, seems unreadable to me. I carry off the fourth without conviction.

*

One can be proud of what one has done, but one should be much prouder of what one has not done. Such pride has yet to be invented.

*

After an evening in his company, you were exhausted, for the necessity of controlling yourself, of avoiding the slightest allusion likely to wound him — and everything wounded him — ultimately left you depleted, irritated with him and with yourself. You resented having to side with him out of scruples carried to the lowest degree of flattery; you despised yourself for not having exploded instead of letting yourself in for so wearying an exercise in . . . delicacy.

*

We never say of a dog or a rat that it is *mortal*. Why is man alone entitled to this privilege? After all, death is not man's discovery, and it is a sign of fatuity to imagine oneself its unique beneficiary.

*

As memory weakens, the praise that has been lavished upon us fades, too, to the advantage of the censure. And this is just: the praise has rarely been deserved, whereas the censure sheds a certain light on what we did not know about ourselves.

*

If I had been born a Buddhist, I should have remained

one; born a Christian, I ceased being one in early youth when, much more so than today, I would have abounded in the sense of Goethe's blasphemy when he wrote — the very year of his death — to Zelter, "The Cross is the most hideous image on this earth."

*

The essential often appears at the end of a long conversation. The great truths are spoken on the doorstep.

*

What is dated in Proust: those trifles swollen by a dizzying prolixity, the eddies of the Symbolist manner, the accumulation of effects, the poetic saturation. As if Saint-Simon had undergone the influence of the *Précieuses*. No one would read him today.

*

A letter worthy of the name is written in the wake of admiration or outrage — of exaggeration, in short. We realize why a sensible letter is a stillborn one.

*

I have known obtuse writers, even stupid ones. On the other hand, the translators I have managed to approach were more intelligent and more interesting than the authors they translated. After all, it takes more reflection to translate than to "create."

*

Someone regarded as "extraordinary" by his intimates must not furnish proofs against himself. Let him take care not to leave traces, above all not to write, if he ever hopes to seem what he has been for the happy few.

*

For a writer, to change languages is to write a love letter with a dictionary.

*

"I feel you have come to hate what other people think

quite as much as what you think yourself," she told me straightaway, after a long separation. And just as she was leaving, she produced a Chinese fable to prove that nothing can equal the capacity to forget oneself. She, the most *present* being, the creature most charged with interior energy, with energy *tout court,* so closely clamped to her ego, so inconceivably full of herself — by what misunderstanding was she boosting effacement to the point of imagining that she offered a perfect example of it?

*

Ill-mannered beyond permissible limits, miserly, dirty, insolent, cunning, sensitive to the slightest nuance, shrieking with delight over any excess, any joke, scheming and slanderous — everything in him was charm and repulsion. A swine one regrets.

*

The mission of Everyman is to fulfill the lie he incarnates, to succeed in being no more than an exhausted illusion.

*

Lucidity: a permanent martyrdom, an unimaginable tour de force.

*

Those who want to tell us scandalous confidences count quite cynically on our curiosity to satisfy their need, which is to make a show of secrets. They know perfectly well, at the same time, that we will be too jealous of them to betray them.

*

Only music can create an indestructible complicity between two persons. A passion is perishable, it decays, like everything that partakes of life, whereas music is of an essence superior to life and, of course, to death.

*

If I have no taste for Mystery, it is because everything seems inexplicable — because I live on the inexplicable, gorged with it.

*

X reproached me for being a spectator, for not getting involved, for loathing the new. "But I don't want to change anything," I answered. He did not grasp the meaning of my reply. He took it for modesty.

*

It has been justly observed that a philosophical jargon ages just as rapidly as argot. Why? The first is too artificial; the second, too vital. Two ruinous excesses.

*

He has been living his last days for months, for years, and speaks of his end in the past tense. A posthumous existence. I am amazed that, eating virtually nothing, he manages to survive: "My body and my soul have taken so much time and so much effort to get together that they can't succeed in separating." If he doesn't have the voice of a dying man, it is because it has been so long now that he is no longer "in life." "I am a snuffed candle" is the most accurate thing he said about his latest metamorphosis. When I suggested the possibility of a miracle, "It would take more than one" was his reply.

*

After fifteen years of absolute solitude, Saint Seraphinus of Sarow would exclaim, in the presence of any visitor at all, "O my joy!" Who, continually rubbing up against his kind, would be so extravagant as to greet them thus?

*

To survive a destructive book is no less painful for the reader than for the author.

*

We must be in a state of receptivity — that is, of physical weakness — for words to touch us, to insinuate themselves into us and there begin a sort of career.

*

To be called a deicide is the most flattering insult that can be addressed to an individual or to a people.

*

Orgasm is a paroxysm; despair, too. One lasts an instant; the other, a lifetime.

*

She had the profile of Cleopatra. Seven years later, she might just as well be begging on the street. Enough to cure you forever of idolatry, of any craving to seek the *unfathomable* in a pair of eyes, in a smile, etc.

*

Let us be reasonable. No one can see through everything completely. Nor, without universal disillusion, can there be universal knowledge, either.

*

What is not heartrending is superfluous, at least in music.

*

Brahms represents "*die Melancholie des Unvermögens,*" the melancholy of impotence, according to Nietzsche. This judgment, passed on the brink of the philosopher's collapse, forever dims its luster.

*

To have accomplished nothing and to die overworked.

*

Those imbecilic people one passes — how have they come to this? And how to imagine such a spectacle in antiquity — in Athens, for example? One moment of acute lucidity among these damned souls, and all illusions collapse.

*

The more you loathe humanity, the riper you are for God, for a dialogue with no one.

*

Extreme fatigue goes quite as far as ecstasy, except that with fatigue you *descend* toward the extremities of knowledge.

*

Just as the advent of the Crucified One has cut history in two, in the same way this night has severed my life.

*

Everything seems debased and futile once the music stops. You understand that music can be hated, and one is tempted to identify its absolute status with fraudulence. This is because we must react at any cost against it *when we love it too much*. No one has realized this danger better than Tolstoy, for he knew that music could do with him as it liked. Hence he began execrating it out of fear of becoming its plaything.

*

Renunciation is the only kind of action that is not degrading.

*

Can we imagine a city dweller who does not have the soul of a murderer?

*

To love only the indefinite thought that never reaches words, and the instantaneous thought that lives by words alone: divagation and boutade.

*

A young German asks me for one franc. I begin a conversation with him and learn that he has traveled round the world, that he has been to India, whose beggars he likes to think he resembles. Yet one does not belong with impunity to a didactic nation. I watch him solicit: he looks as if he had taken courses in mendicancy.

＊

Nature, in search of a formula likely to content everyone, let her choice fall on death, which — as was to be expected — has satisfied no one.

＊

Heraclitus has a Delphic side and a textbook side, a mixture of lightning-bolt perceptions and the primer: a man of inspiration and a schoolteacher. A pity he did not drop learning, did not always think *outside* learning!

＊

I have so often stormed against any form of action that to manifest myself in any way at all seems an imposture, even a betrayal.

— Yet you go on breathing.

— Yes, I do everything that is done. *But* . . .

＊

What a judgment upon the living, if it is true, as has been maintained, that what dies has never existed!

＊

While he described his projects to me, I listened to him without being able to forget that he would not survive the week. What madness on his part to speak of the future, of *his* future! But once I had left, once I was outside, how to avoid thinking that after all, the difference was not so great between the mortal and the moribund? The absurdity of making plans is only a little more obvious in the second case.

＊

We always date ourselves by our admirations. As soon as we cite anyone but Homer or Shakespeare, we risk seeming old-fashioned or dotty.

＊

It is just possible to imagine God speaking French. Christ, never. His words do not function in a language so ill at ease in the naive or the sublime.

*

So long to have questioned ourselves about man! Impossible to carry the taste of the morbid further.

*

Does fury come from God or from the Devil? From both; otherwise, how explain that our rage dreams of galaxies to pulverize and that it is inconsolable at having nothing but this wretched planet within reach?

*

We go to such lengths — why? To become again what we were before we were.

X, who has failed in everything, complained in my presence of not having a destiny.

— Oh yes, certainly you do. The sequence of your failures is so remarkable that it seems to reveal a providential plan.

*

Woman mattered as long as she simulated shame, reserve. What inadequacy she reveals by no longer playing the game! Already she is worth nothing, now that she resembles us. Thus vanishes one of the last lies that made existence tolerable.

*

To love one's neighbor is inconceivable. Does one ask a virus to love another virus?

*

The only notable events of a life are its rifts. And it is they that are the last to fade from our memory.

*

When I learned he was quite impermeable to both Dostoyevsky and music, I refused — for all his great virtues — to meet him. I much prefer a slightly backward type, sensitive to one or the other.

*

The fact that life has no meaning is a reason to live — moreover, the only one.

*

Since day after day I have lived in the company of Suicide, it would be unjust and ungrateful on my part to denigrate it. What could be healthier, what could be more natural? What is neither healthy nor natural is the frantic appetite to exist — a grave flaw, a flaw par excellence, my flaw.

4

Valéry Facing His Idols

*

IT IS A MISFORTUNE for an author to be understood, as Valéry was in his lifetime, as he has been subsequently. Was he so simple, then, so *penetrable?* Certainly not. But he was imprudent enough to furnish too many details about himself and his work; he revealed himself, gave himself away, supplied any number of keys, and dissolved a good many of those misunderstandings indispensable to a writer's secret prestige. Instead of leaving the labor of decipherment to others, he took it upon himself; he made a kind of vice out of the craving for self-disclosure. This singularly facilitated the commentators' task: by initiating them from the start into his essential actions and preoccupations, he invited them to ruminate not so much upon his work as upon the remarks he himself had made about it. Henceforth the Valerian question would be whether, on this or that point concerning him, he had been the victim of an illusion or, on the contrary, of an *excessive* clairvoyance — in either case, of a judgment dislocated from reality. Not only was Valéry his own commentator, but indeed all his works are merely a more or less camouflaged autobiography, an adept introspection, a *diary* of his mind, a promotion of his experiences — any of his experiences — to the rank of intellectual event, an assault upon anything *unconsidered* that might be within him, a rebellion against his depths.

To be capable of dismantling the mechanism of everything, since everything is mechanism, a sum of contraptions, artifices, or, to use a more honorable word, operations; to deal with the springs and ratchets, to become a watchmaker, to see *inside,* to cease to be duped — that is what counts in his eyes. Man, as Valéry conceives him, is valued only for the degree of lucidity he may attain, his capacity for non-consent. This demand for lucidity suggests the level of *awakening* that any mental experience supposes and that is determined by the answer to the crucial question, "How far have you gone in the perception of unreality?"

We might trace in some detail the parallel between a quest for lucidity deliberately *this side* of the absolute, as we find it in Valéry, and a quest for awakening with a view to the absolute, which is, strictly speaking, the mystic way. In both procedures, what is involved is an exacerbated consciousness eager to shake off the illusions trailing after it. Any pitiless analyst, any betrayer of appearances, a fortiori any "nihilist," is merely a *blocked* mystic, and this only because he is reluctant to grant a content to his lucidity, to inflect it toward salvation by associating it with an enterprise transcending it. Valéry was too contaminated by positivism to conceive any cult but that of lucidity *for its own sake.*

"I confess I have made my mind into an idol, but I have found nothing else that would serve." Valéry would never get over the amazement produced in him by the spectacle of that mind. He admired only men who deified theirs, and whose aspirations were so excessive that they could only fascinate or dismay. What seduced him in Mallarmé was the *madman,* the fanatic who had written to Verlaine, in 1885, "I have always imagined and attempted *something else,* with an alchemist's patience, ready to sacrifice all vanity and all satisfaction, the way such men once burned up their own furniture and the very rafters of their house in order to feed the furnace of the Great Work. Which is what? It is hard to say: a book, quite simply, in many volumes, a book that really is a book, architectural and premeditated, and not a collection of chance inspirations, however marvelous. . . . I shall go further and say The Book, convinced after all that there is only one." As early as 1867 he had formulated, in a letter to Cazalis, the same grandiose and insane aspiration: ". . . it would cause me a real pang to enter into the supreme Disappearance without having completed my work, which is The Work, the Great Work, as the alchemists, our ancestors, used to call it."

To create a work that *rivals* the world, that is not its reflection but its double — this notion Mallarmé derived not so much from the alchemists as from Hegel, that Hegel whom he knew only indirectly, from Villiers, who had read the philosopher just enough to be able to quote him on occasion and to call him, pompously, "the reconstructor of the Universe," a formula that must have struck Mallarmé, since The Book specifically intends the reconstruction of the Universe. But this notion could also have been inspired by his frequentation of music, by the theories of the period derived from Schopenhauer and propagated by the Wagnerians, who made music the one art capable of translating the essence of the world. Moreover,

Wagner's enterprise itself could suggest great dreams and lead to megalomania quite as easily as alchemy or Hegelianism. A musician — especially a fecund one — can aspire to the role of demiurge; but how could a poet — and a poet delicate to the point of sterility — undertake such a thing without absurdity or madness? All of which partakes of *divagation,* to use a word Mallarmé was fond of. And it was precisely in this aspect that he beguiled, that he convinced. Valéry imitates and extends him when he speaks of that *Commedia* of the intellect he intended to write some day. The dream of excess leads to absolute illusion. When, on November 3, 1897, Mallarmé showed Valéry the corrected proofs of *Un Coup de dés* and asked him, "Don't you find this an act of madness?," the madman was not Mallarmé but the Valéry who, in a fit of sublimity, would write that in the strange typography of that poem the author had attempted "to raise a page to the power of the starry heavens." To assign oneself a task impossible to realize and even to define, to crave vigor when one is corroded by the subtlest of anemias — in all this there is a touch of theater, a desire to deceive oneself, to live intellectually beyond one's means, a will to legend and to defeat, for at a certain level the man of failure is incomparably more captivating than the one who has merely achieved success.

We are increasingly interested not in what an author says but in what he may have meant, not in his actions but in his projects, less in his actual work than in the work he dreamed of. If Mallarmé intrigues us, it is because he fulfills the conditions of the writer who is unrealized in relation to the disproportionate ideal he has assigned himself, an ideal so disproportionate that we are sometimes inclined to call a man naive or insincere who in reality is merely hallucinated — obsessed. We are adepts of the work that is aborted, abandoned halfway through, impossible to complete, undermined by its very requirements. The strange thing in this case is that the work was not even begun, for of The Book, that rival of the Universe, there remains virtually no revealing clue; it is doubtful that its structure was outlined in the notes Mallarmé destroyed, those that have survived being unworthy of our attention. Mallarmé: an impulse of thought, a thought that was never actualized, that snagged itself on the potential, on the unreal, disengaged from all actions, superior to all objects, even to all concepts — an expectation of thought. And what he, enemy of the vague, ultimately expressed is just that expectation which is nothing but vagueness itself. Yet such vagueness, the space of excess, affords a positive aspect: it permits imagining *big*. It was by dreaming of The Book that Mallarmé achieved the unique: had he been more *reasonable,* he would have left us a mediocre body of work. We can say as much of Valéry, who is the result of his almost mythological vision of his faculties, of what he might have extracted from them if he had had the chance or the time to put them to actual use. Are not his *Cahiers* the bric-a-brac of The Book that he, too, wanted to write? He went further than Mallarmé but realized no better than he a scheme that requires persistence and a great invulnerability to boredom, to that wound which, by his own admission, continually tormented him. Yet such boredom is discontinuity itself, impatience with any sustained, grounded reasoning, a pulverized obsession, the horror of system (The Book could only have been a system, a *total* system), horror of an idea's insistence, of its *duration;* boredom is also the non sequitur, the fragment, the note, the *cahier* — in other words, dilettantism consequent upon a lack of vitality, and also upon a fear of being or of seeming *deep*. Valéry's attack on Pascal might be explained by a reaction of modesty: is it not indecent to display one's secrets, one's lacerations, one's abysses? Let us not forget that for a Mediterranean such as Valéry the *senses* mattered, and that for him the basic categories were not what is and what is not, but what is not at all and what might exist, Nothingness and the Apparent; *being* as such lacked dimension in his eyes, and even significance.

Neither Mallarmé nor Valéry was equipped to confront The Book. Before them, Poe would have been able both to conceive such a project and to undertake it, indeed, he did undertake it, *Eureka* being a kind of limit-work, an extremity, an end, a colossal and *realized* dream. "I have solved the secret of the Universe"; "I no longer desire to live, since I have written *Eureka*" — these are exclamations Mallarmé would have loved to utter; he had no right to do so, not even after that magnificent impasse, *Un Coup de dés*. Baudelaire had called Poe a "hero" of letters; Mallarmé went further and called him "the absolute literary case." No one today would assent to such a judgment, but that is of no consequence, for each individual (like each epoch) possesses *reality* only by his exaggerations, by his capacity to overestimate — by his gods. The sequence of philosophical or literary fashions testifies to an irresistible need to worship: who has not put in time as a hagiographer? A skeptic will always manage to venerate someone more skeptical than himself. Even in the eighteenth century, when disparagement became an institution, the "decadence of admiration" was not to be so general as Montesquieu had supposed.

For Valéry, the theme treated in *Eureka* resulted in

literature: "Cosmogony is a literary genre of a remarkable persistence and of an amazing variety, one of the oldest genres there is." He believed as much of history and even of philosophy, "a special literary genre characterized by certain subjects and by the frequency of certain terms and certain forms." It may be said that with the exception of the positive sciences, everything came down to literature for him, to something dubious if not contemptible. But where are we to find someone more *literary* than he, someone in whom attention to the word, idolatry of utterance, is more intensely sustained? A Narcissus turned against himself, he disdained the only activity in accord with his nature: *predestined* to the Word, he was essentially a litterateur, and it was this litterateur he wanted to smother, to destroy; unable to do so, he took his revenge on the literature he so maligned. Such would be the psychological schema of his relations with it.

Eureka did not affect Valéry's development. On the other hand, *The Philosophy of Composition* was a major event, a crucial encounter. Everything he was subsequently to believe about the mechanism of the poetic act is there. We can imagine the delight with which he must have read that the composition of "The Raven" could in no way be attributed to chance or to intuition, and that the poem had been conceived with "the precision and the rigorous logic of a mathematical problem." Another of Poe's declarations, this time from *Marginalia* (CXVIII), must have gratified him no less: "It is the curse of a certain order of mind, that it can never rest satisfied with the consciousness of its ability to do a thing. Still less is it content with doing it. It must both know and show how it was done."

The Philosophy of Composition was, on Poe's part, a mere hoax; all Valéry comes out of a . . . naive reading, the idolatry of a text in which a poet dupes his credulous readers. Such youthful enthusiasm for so basically anti-poetic a demonstration proves that initially, in his depths, Valéry was no poet, for his whole being should have bridled in protest at this cold and pitiless dismantling of rapture, this indictment of the most elementary poetic reflex, of poetry's very raison d'être; but no doubt he needed such cunning incrimination, such a rebuke to any spontaneous creation, in order to justify, to *excuse,* his own lack of spontaneity. What could be more reassuring than this studious exposition of *devices!* Here was a catechism not for poets but for versifiers, and one that would necessarily flatter in Valéry that virtuoso aspect, that yen for one-upmanship in reflection, for art to the second degree, for the art *within* art, that religion of taking pains, along with that will to be, at every moment, outside of what one creates, outside of any intoxication, poetic or otherwise. Only a maniac of lucidity could savor this cynical reversion to the sources of the poem contradicting all the laws of literary production, this infinitely meticulous premeditation, these outrageous acrobatics from which Valéry drew the first article of his poetic credo. He erected into a theory and proposed as a model his very incapacity to be a poet naturally; he bound himself to a technique in order to conceal his congenital lacunae; he set — an inexpiable offense! — poetics above poetry. We can legitimately suppose that all his theses would be quite different had he been capable of producing a less elaborated oeuvre. He promoted the Difficult *out of impotence:* all his requirements are those of an artist and not of a poet. What in Poe was merely a game is in Valéry a dogma, a literary dogma — that is, an *accepted* fiction. As a good technician, he attempted to rehabilitate method and métier at the expense of *talent*. From any and every theory — it is art I am speaking of — he was concerned to extract the least poetic conclusion, and it is to that conclusion he would cling, beguiled as he was (to the point of obnubilation) by *praxis,* by invention stripped of fatality, of the ineluctable, of destiny. He always believed one might be other than one is, and always wanted to be other than he was, as is evidenced by that gnawing regret of his at not being a scientist, a regret that inspired him to a good many extravagances, especially in aesthetics; it was also this regret that inspired his condescension toward literature — as if he debased himself by speaking of it, and merely deigned to trifle with verses. As a matter of fact, he did not trifle with them, he *practiced* them, as he specifically said so many times. At least the non-poet in him, keeping him from mingling poetry and prose, from trying to create, like the Symbolists, poetry at all costs and on all occasions, saved him from that scourge: any prose that is too ostensibly poetic. When we approach a mind as subtle as Valéry's, we experience a rare pleasure in discovering its illusions and its flaws, which, if they are not obvious, are no less real, absolute lucidity being incompatible with existence, with the exercise of breathing. And we must admit, a disabused mind, whatever its degree of emancipation from the world, lives more or less within the unbreathable.

Poe and Mallarmé *exist* for Valéry; Leonardo, evidently, is but a pretext, a name and nothing more, a figure entirely constructed, a monster who possesses all the powers one lacks and longs for. He answers that need to see oneself fulfilled, realized in some imagined person who represents the ideal epitome of all the illusions one has created about oneself: a hero who has conquered one's own impossibilities, who has delivered one from one's limits, transcending them *in one's place*. . . .

The *Introduction to the Method of Leonardo da Vinci*, which dates from 1894, proves that Valéry, in his initial phases, was perfect — that is, perfectly ripe — as a writer: the chore of self-improvement, of making progress, he was spared from the start. His case is not without analogies to that of his compatriot who could declare at Saint-Helena, "War is a singular art: I can assure you I have waged sixty battles, and I have learned no more than I already knew after the first." Valéry, at the end of his career, could maintain that he, too, *knew* everything, from his very first efforts, and that with regard to demands upon himself and his work, he was no more advanced at sixty than at twenty. At an age when everyone gropes and apes everyone else, he had found his manner, his style, his form of thought. He would still admire, no doubt, but *as a master*. Like all perfect minds, his was *limited* — that is, confined within certain themes from which he could not escape. It was perhaps in reaction against himself, against his evident frontiers, that he was so intrigued by the phenomenon of a universal mind, by the scarcely conceivable possibility of a multiplicity of talents that flourish without harming each other, that cohabit without canceling each other out. He could not fail to *encounter* Leonardo; yet Leibnitz made a deeper impression. No doubt. But to confront Leibnitz required not only the scientific competence and knowledge that he lacked, but an impersonal curiosity of which he was incapable. With Leonardo, symbol of a civilization, a universe, or whatever, the arbitrary and the casual were much more comfortable. If one quoted him now and then, it was only in order to talk more readily

about oneself, about one's own tastes and distastes, to
settle accounts with the philosophers by invoking a name
that, all by itself, summed up faculties none of them ever
combined. For Valéry, the problems philosophy approached and the way it expressed them came down to
"abuses of language," to false problems, fruitless and interchangeable, lacking all rigor, verbal or intrinsic. To him
it seemed that an idea was denatured as soon as the philosophers got hold of it; even that thought itself was vi-
tiated upon contact with them. His horror of philosophic
jargon is so convincing, so contagious, that one shares it
forever after, so that one can no longer read a *serious*
philosopher except with suspicion or distaste, henceforth
rejecting any falsely mysterious or learned term. Most philosophy boils down to a crime of *lèse-langage,* a crime
against the Word. Any professional expression — any
expression of the *schools* — must be proscribed and identified with a misdemeanor. Anyone who, in order to settle
a difficulty or solve a problem, invents a high-sounding,
pretentious word, indeed a word at all, is unconsciously
dishonest. In a letter to F. Brunot, Valéry once wrote, "It
takes more intelligence to do without a word than to introduce one." If we were to translate the philosophers'
lucubrations into *normal* language, what would be left of
them? The enterprise would be ruinous for the vast majority. But we must immediately add that it would also be
ruinous for most writers, singularly so for a Valéry: if we
stripped his prose of its luster, reduced one or another of
his thoughts to skeletal contours, what would it still be
worth? He too was the dupe of language, of *another* language, one more real, more *existent,* it is true. He did not
invent words, of course, but he lived in a quasi-absolute
fashion within his own language, so that his superiority

over the philosophers was precisely that he participated in less of an unreality than they. By criticizing them so severely he showed that he, too — ordinarily so disabused — could be carried away, could be deluded. A total disenchantment, moreover, had stifled in him not only "the man of thought," as he sometimes called himself, but — a more serious loss — the *jongleur,* the histrion of syllables. Fortunately he did not achieve that "imperturbable clairvoyance" he dreamed of; otherwise his "silence" might have lasted until his death.

Considered further, his aversion to the philosophers has something impure about it; as a matter of fact, he was *obsessed* with them, could not be indifferent to them, pursued them with an irony bordering on dyspepsia. All his life he forswore any attempt to build a system; yet he nourished — as with regard to science — a more or less conscious regret for the system he could not build. The hatred of philosophy is always suspect: as if one does not forgive oneself for not having been a philosopher, and, in order to mask that regret, or that incapacity, mistreats those who, less scrupulous or more gifted, had the luck to construct that improbable little universe, a well-articulated philosophical doctrine. That a "thinker" should regret the philosopher he might have been is understandable; less so, that this regret should still encumber a poet: we are reminded once again of Mallarmé, since The Book could only be the work of a philosopher. Glamour of rigor, of thought *without charm!* If the poets are so sensitive to it, it is out of a sort of mortification at living quite shamelessly as parasites of the Improbable.

Academic philosophy is one thing; metaphysics is another. We might have expected Valéry to show a certain indulgence toward the latter; nothing of the kind. He denounces it quite insidiously and comes close to treating it — as does the logical positivism to which he is in many respects so close — as a "disease of language." He even made it a point of honor to ridicule all metaphysical anxiety; the torments of a Pascal inspire him to the reflections of an engineer: "No revelations for Leonardo. No abyss opens at his side. For him, an abyss suggests a bridge. An abyss might be useful for experiments involving some huge mechanical bird." When we read remarks so unforgivably casual, we can have only one reaction: to *avenge* Pascal on the spot. What was the sense of blaming him for abandoning the sciences, when that abandonment was the result of a spiritual *awakening* much more important than the scientific discoveries he might have made subsequently? In the scale of the absolute, the Pascalian perplexities on the confines of prayer weigh more heavily than any secret wrested from the external world. Any *objective* conquest presupposes an interior retreat. When man has achieved the goal he has assigned himself — to enslave Creation — then he will be completely empty: god and ghost. Scientism, that great illusion of modern times, Valéry espoused without reservations, without second thoughts. Is it a mere accident that in his youth in Montpellier, he occupied the bedroom lived in, years before, by Auguste Comte, theoretician and prophet of all scientism?

Of all the superstitions, the least original is that of science. No doubt we can engage in scientific activity, but enthusiasm for it, *when we are not on the team,* is embarrassing, to say the least. Valéry himself created his poet-mathematician legend. And everyone accepted it, though he himself acknowledged that he was merely "an unhappy lover of the loveliest of the sciences," and once declared to Frédéric Lefèvre that as a young man he had failed to become a navel cadet because of an "absolute incomprehension of the mathematical sciences. I didn't understand one iota. For me it was the strangest, most impenetrable, most dismaying thing in the world. No one has ever understood less of the existence and virtually the possibility of even the simplest mathematics than myself in those days." That subsequently he acquired a taste for mathematics is undeniable, but to acquire a taste and to achieve mastery are two very different things. He became interested, either to create for himself a peerless intellectual status (to make himself the hero of a drama at the limit of the mind's powers), or to enter a realm where one is not constantly encountering oneself. "There are no words to express the delight of realizing that a world exists from which the Self is entirely absent." Did Valéry know Sophie Kowalevsky's remark about mathematics? Perhaps an analogous need led him toward a discipline so remote from any form of narcissism. But if we question the existence of this profound necessity for him, his relations with the sciences will suggest the infatuation of those Enlightenment ladies whom he mentions in his preface to the *Persian Letters* and who haunted the laboratories and became fanatics of anatomy or astronomy. We must admit (and praise him for it) that in his way of delivering himself upon the sciences we recognize the tone of a man of the world of the *grande époque,* the last echo of those bygone salons. We might also detect, in his pursuit of the unapproachable, a touch of masochism: to worship, in order to torment oneself, what one will never achieve; to punish oneself for being, in the realm of Knowledge, a mere amateur.

The only problems he confronted as a connoisseur, as an initiate, were those of form or, to be more precise, of writing. "A syntactic genius," Claudel's description of

Mallarmé, applies even better to Valéry, who himself attributes to Mallarmé the faculty of "conceiving and placing above *all works* the conscious possession of the function of language and the sentiment of a superior freedom of expression in regard to which any thought is merely an incident, a particular event." Valéry's cult of rigor goes no further than correctness of terms and a conscious effort toward an *abstract* brilliance of phrase. Rigor of form, and not of substance. *La Jeune Parque* required more than a hundred drafts: the author prided himself upon them, and in them discerned the very symbol of a rigorous enterprise. To leave nothing to the powers of improvisation or inspiration (accursed synonyms in his eyes), to scrutinize words, to weigh them, never to forget that language is the sole, the unique, reality — such is this will-to-expression, carried so far that it turns into a fanaticism about trifles, an exhausting search for infinitesimal precision. Valéry: the galley slave of Nuance.

He went to the extremity of language, where the latter, aerial, dangerously subtle, is no more than a lacy *essence,* a last stage *before* unreality. We cannot conceive of a discourse more refined than his, more marvelously bloodless. Why deny that in many places it is finicky or distinctly precious? He himself held preciosity in high esteem, as this significant avowal testifies: "Who knows if Molière has not cost us a Shakespeare, in casting such ridicule upon *les précieux*?" The trouble with preciosity is that it makes a writer too conscious, too imbued with his superiority over his instrument: by wielding it with such virtuosity, he dispossesses language of all mystery and all vigor. Now, language must *resist;* if it yields, it capitulates utterly to the whims of a prestidigitator, resolved into a series of pirouettes and *trouvailles* in which it constantly triumphs over and divides against itself, to the point of annihilation. Preciosity is the writing of writing: a style that doubles itself and becomes the object of its own quest. It would be abusive to regard Valéry as a *précieux,* but it is just to say that he had *fits and starts* of preciosity — quite natural in someone who perceived nothing *behind* language, no substratum or residue of reality. Only words preserve us from nothingness: such seems to be the *content* of his thought, though *content* is a term he rejected in both its metaphysical and its aesthetic acceptation. The fact remains that he emphatically banked on words and thereby proved he still believed in something. Only if he had finally become detached from them could we have called him a nihilist. In any case, he was too sensitive to the urgency of the life-lie for nihilism. "One would lose courage if one were not sustained by false ideas," said Fontenelle, the writer whom, in the grace he could lend to the slightest idea, Valéry most resembles.

Poetry is *threatened* when poets take too lively a theoretical interest in language and make it into a constant subject of meditation, when they confer upon it an exceptional status that derives less from aesthetics than from theology. The obsession with language, always intense in France, has never been so virulent, and so sterilizing, as it is today: we are not far from promoting the means, the intermediary, of thought into the sole object of thought, even into a substitute for the absolute, not to say for God. There is no vital, fecund thought that encroaches on reality if the word is brutally substituted for the idea, if the vehicle counts more than the load it transports, if the instrument of thought is identified with thought itself. If we are truly to think, thought must *adhere* to the mind; if it becomes independent of the mind, exterior to it, the mind is shackled from the start, idles, and has but one resource left — itself — instead of relying on the world for its substance or its pretexts. The writer must guard against reflecting excessively upon language, must avoid making it the substance of his obsessions, must never forget that the important works have been created *despite* language. A Dante was obsessed by what he had to say, not by the saying of it. For a long time — indeed forever, one is tempted to say — French literature seems to have succumbed to the enchantment, and to the despotism, of the Word, hence its tenuity, its fragility, its extreme delicacy, and also it mannerism. Mallarmé and Valéry crown a tradition and prefigure an exhaustion; both are terminal symptoms of a *grammarian* nation. One linguist could even declare that Mallarmé treated French like a dead language and that "he might never have heard it spoken." To which we may add that there was a touch of the poseur in him, of the "ironic and tricky Parisian" Claudel had observed, a suspicion of "charlatanism" (though of the highest order), the lassitude of a man who has seen through everything — features we shall recognize, to a somewhat more marked degree, in the Valéry of "the indefinite refusal to be anything in particular," key-formula of his intellectual enterprise, leading principle, rule, and motto of his mind. And in effect Valery will never be *entire,* will not identify himself with beings or with things, will be *off to one side,* marginal to everything, and this not because of some malaise of a metaphysical order but out of an excess of reflection on the operations, on the functioning, of consciousness. The ruling idea, the idea that gives meaning to all his efforts, circles that distance which consciousness takes with regard to itself, that *consciousness of consciousness,* as it chiefly appears in the

Note and Digression of 1919, his "philosophic" master-piece, in which, seeking some *constant* amid our sensations and our judgments, he finds it not in our changing personality but in the pure ego, "universal pronoun," "appellation of *that* which has no relation to a face," "which has no name," "which has no history," and which is in short merely a phenomenon of exacerbated consciousness, merely a limit-existence, quasi-fictive, stripped of any fixed content and without any relation to the psychological subject. This sterile ego, a summa of refusals, quintessence of nothing, conscious void (not consciousness of the void but a void that knows itself and rejects the accidents and vicissitudes of the contingent subject), this ego, last stage of lucidity, of a lucidity decanted and purified of any complicity with objects or events, is located at the antipodes of the Ego — infinite productivity, cosmogonic force — as German Romanticism had conceived it.

Consciousness intervenes in our actions only to frustrate their execution; consciousness is a perpetual interrogation of life, it is perhaps the ruin of life. *Bewusstsein als Verhängnis* (Consciousness as Fatality) is the title of a book published in Germany between the two world wars, whose author, drawing the consequences of his vision of the world, committed suicide. There is, as far as we can see, in the phenomenon of consciousness a dramatic and deadly dimension that did not escape Valéry (we need merely recall the "murderous lucidity" of *Dance and the Soul*), but he could not emphasize it too much without contradicting his usual theories about the beneficent role of consciousness in literary creation, as opposed to the suspect character of trace. His entire poetics, what is it but the apotheosis of consciousness? If he had lingered too long over the tension between the Vital and the Conscious, he would have had to reverse the scale of values that he had set up and that he remained faithful to throughout his career.

The effort to define oneself, to bear down upon one's own mental operations, Valéry took for true knowledge. But to know *oneself* is not *to know*, or rather is only a variety of knowing. Valéry always confused *knowledge* and *clear-sightedness*. Indeed the will to be clear-sighted, to be inhumanly disabused, is accompanied for him by an ill-concealed pride: he knows himself and admires himself for knowing himself. Let us be fair: he does not admire his mind, he admires himself as Mind. His narcissism, inseparable from what he called "emotions" and the "pathos" of the intellect, is not a narcissism of *journaux intimes,* it is not the attachment to the self as a *unique* aberration, nor is it the ego of those who like to *hear themselves,* psychologically speaking; no, it is an abstract ego, far from the complacencies of introspection or the impurities of psychoanalysis. Note that the flaw of Narcissus was not consubstantial with him: how else explain that the sole realm in which posterity has strikingly vindicated Valéry is that of political considerations and prophecies? History, an idol he was concerned to demolish, is largely what ensures that he will last, that he will continue to be *present.* For it is his observations concerning History that are quoted most frequently — an irony he would perhaps have enjoyed. Doubts are cast on his poems, his poetics are rejected, but increasingly we set store by the moralist and the analyst attentive to events. This lover of himself had the stuff of an extrovert. Appearances, one feels, did not displease him; nothing in him assumed a morbid, profound, supremely intimate aspect; even the Nothingness he inherited from Mallarmé was merely a fascination exempt from vertigo, and never opened out onto horror or ecstasy. In one of the Upanishads, it is said that "the essence of man is speech, the essence of speech is the hymn." Valéry would have assented to the first assertion and denied the second. It is in this assent and this denial that we must seek the key to his accomplishments and to his limits.

1970

5

The Lure of Disillusion

*

I T IS NEVER ideas we should speak of, only sensations and visions — for ideas do not proceed from our entrails; ideas are never truly *ours*.

*

Glum sky: my mind masquerading as the firmament.

*

Ravaged by boredom, that cyclone in slow motion.

*

There exists, I grant you, a clinical depression, upon which certain remedies occasionally have an effect; but there exists another kind, a melancholy underlying our very outbursts of gaiety and accompanying us everywhere, without leaving us *alone* for a single moment. And there is nothing that can rid us of this lethal omnipresence: the self forever confronting itself.

*

I assure this foreign poet, who after hesitating among several capitals has decided on ours, that he has chosen well, that here he will find, among other advantages, that of starving to death without troubling a single soul. To encourage him further, I explain that here failure is so normal that it is a kind of Open Sesame. This detail provided the finishing touch, judging from the gleam I detected in his eyes.

*

"The very fact that you have reached the age you have proves that life has a meaning," I was told by a friend I hadn't seen in over thirty years. This remark often comes back to me, more striking each time, though it was made by someone who has always found a meaning in everything.

*

For Mallarmé, who claimed he was doomed to permanent insomnia, sleep was not a "real need" but a "favor." Only a great poet could allow himself the luxury of such an insanity.

*

Insomnia appears to spare the animals. If we kept them from sleeping for a few weeks, a radical change would occur in their nature and their behavior. They would experience hitherto unknown sensations, the kind that seemed to be specifically human. Let us wreck the animal kingdom, if we want it to overtake and replace us.

*

In each letter I send to a Japanese friend, I have got into the habit of recommending one or another work by Brahms. She has just written that she is leaving a Tokyo clinic where she was taken by ambulance for having excessively sacrificed to my idol. I wonder which trio, which sonata was responsible. It doesn't matter. Whatever induces collapse is thereby deserving of being listened to.

*

There is no speculation about Knowledge, no *Erkennt-nistheorie* in which so many philosophers, German or otherwise, revel, that offers the slightest homage to Fatigue as such — the state likeliest to lead us to the heart of the matter. This neglect or this ingratitude definitively discredits our philosophy.

*

A stroll through Montparnasse Cemetery. All, young or old, made plans. They make no more. Strengthened by their example, I swear as a good pupil, returning, never to make any myself — ever. Undeniably beneficial outing.

*

I ponder C., for whom drinking in a café was the sole reason to exist. One day when I was eloquently vaunting Buddhism to him, he replied, "Well, yes, nirvana, all right, but not without a café." We all have some mania or other that keeps us from unconditionally accepting supreme happiness.

*

Reading Madame Périer's testimony — specifically, the passage in which she tells how her brother Pascal, from the age of eighteen, by his own admission never spent a single day without suffering — I was so astounded that I stuffed my fist into my mouth to keep from crying out. This was in a public library. I was, it is worth noting, eighteen myself. What a presentiment, but also what madness, and what presumption!

*

To rid oneself of life is to deprive oneself of the pleasure of deriding it. (The one possible answer to someone who informs you of his intention to be done with it all.)

*

"Being never disappoints," declares a philosopher. Then what does? Certainly not nonbeing, by definition incapable of disappointing. This advantage, so irritating to our philosopher, must have led him to promulgate so flagrant a countertruth.

*

The interesting thing about friendship is that it is — almost as much as love — an inexhaustible source of disappointment and outrage, thereby of fruitful surprises it would be madness to try to do without.

*

The surest means of not losing your mind on the spot: remembering that everything is unreal, and will remain so . . .

*

He offers me an unconscious hand. I ask him many questions and lose my courage in the face of his outrageously laconic replies. Not a single one of those useless words so necessary to dialogue. Dialogue indeed! Speech is a sign of life, and that is why the chattering lunatic is closer to us than the tongue-tied half-wit.

*

No possible defense against a flatterer. You cannot agree with him without absurdity; nor can you contradict him and turn your back. You act as if he were telling the truth, you let yourself be sent up because you don't know how to react. He of course believes you are taken in, that he has you where he wants you, and enjoys his triumph without your being able to open his eyes. Generally he is a future enemy who will take his revenge for having prostrated himself before you — a disguised aggressor who ponders his blows while he pours out his hyperboles.

*

The most effective method for making loyal friends is to congratulate them upon their failures.

*

This thinker has taken refuge in prolixity as others do in stupor.

*

When you have circled around a subject for a certain amount of time, you can immediately offer a judgment on any work that relates to it. I have just opened a book on the gnostics, and I immediately perceived that it was quite unreliable. Yet I read only one sentence and am only a dilettante, an incompetent in such matters.

Now imagine an absolute specialist, a monster — God, for example: whatever we do must to Him seem botched, even our inimitable successes, even those that ought to humiliate and embarrass Him.

*

Between Genesis and Apocalypse imposture reigns. It is important to know this, for once assimilated, such dizzying evidence renders all formulas for wisdom superfluous.

*

If you have had the weakness to write a book, you will not fail to admire that Hasidic rabbi who abandoned the project of writing one since he was not sure he could do so exclusively for the pleasure of his Creator.

*

If the Hour of Disappointment were to sound for everyone at the same time, we should see an entirely new version, either of paradise or of hell.

*

Impossible to enter into a *dialogue* with physical pain.

*

To withdraw indefinitely into oneself, like God after the six days. Let us imitate Him, on this point at least.

*

The light of dawn is the true, primordial light. Each time I observe it, I bless my sleepless nights, which afford me an occasion to witness the spectacle of the Beginning. Yeats calls it "sensuous" — a fine discovery, and anything but obvious.

*

Learning that he was going to marry soon, I decided to conceal my amazement by a generality: "Everything is compatible with everything." To which he replied, "You're right, since man is compatible with woman."

*

A flame traverses the blood. To go over to the other side, circumventing death.

*

That favorable look one assumes on the occasion of a blow of fate. . . .

*

At the climax of a performance superfluous to specify, one longs to exclaim *"Consummatum est."* The clichés of the Gospels, and singularly of the Passion, are always good to have at hand for those moments when you might imagine you could do without them.

*

Skeptical observations, so rare in the Fathers of the Church, are today regarded as *modern*. Obviously, since Christianity, having played its part — which at its beginnings heralded its end — is now a subject of delectation.

*

Each time I see a filthy, raving, drunken bum, prostrate with his bottle in the gutter, I think of a future humanity experimenting with its future, and pulling it off.

*

Though seriously deranged, he utters nothing but

banalities. Occasionally a remark that borders on cretin-
ism and genius. Dislocation of the mind must indeed serve
some purpose.

*

When you imagine you have reached a certain degree
of detachment, you regard as histrionic all zealots, including the founders of religions. But doesn't detachment, too,
have a histrionics of its own? If actions are mummery, the
very refusal of action is one as well. Yet a noble mummery.

*

His nonchalance leaves me perplexed and admiring. He
shows no haste, follows no direction, generates enthusiasm for no subject. As if at birth he had swallowed a tran-
quilizer whose effect has never worn off, and which allows
him to preserve his indestructible smile.

*

Pity the man who, having exhausted his reserves of
scorn, no longer knows what to feel about others, about
himself!

*

Cut off from the world, having broken with all his
friends, he read me — with an almost indispensable Russian accent, given the situation — the beginning of the
Book of Books. Reaching the moment where Adam gets
himself expelled from paradise, he fell silent, dreamily
staring into the distance while I thought to myself, more
or less distinctly, that after millennia of false hopes, humanity, furious at having cheated, would finally receive
the meaning of the curse and thereby make itself worthy
of its first ancestor.

*

If Meister Eckhart is the only "scholastic" who is still
readable, it is because in him profundity is matched by

charm, by *glamour* — an advantage rare in periods of intense faith.

*

Listening to some oratorio, how can we admit that such beseechings, such poignant effusions, conceal no reality and concern no one, that there is nothing behind them, and that they must vanish forever *into thin air?*

*

In a Hindu village where the inhabitants wove cashmere shawls, a European manufacturer made an extended stay while examining the weavers' unconscious methods. Having studied them thoroughly, he revealed them to these simple souls, who thereupon lost all spontaneity and became, indeed, very poor workers. Excess of deliberation frustrates all actions. To expatiate upon sexuality is to sabotage it altogether. Eroticism, scourge of deliquescent societies, is an offense against instinct, an organized impotence. We do not reflect with impunity upon exploits that dispense with reflection. Orgasm has never been a philosophical event.

*

My dependence on climate will forever keep me from acknowledging the autonomy of the will. Meteorology determines the color of my thoughts. One cannot be more crudely determinist than I am, but I am helpless to alter the case. . . . Once I forget I have a body, I believe in freedom, but I immediately abandon such belief when my body calls me back to order and imposes its miseries and its whims. Montesquieu belongs here: "Happiness or misery consists in a certain arrangement of organs."

*

Had I done what I intended, would I be happier today? Certainly not. Having set out to travel far, toward the extremity of myself, I have begun, on the way, to doubt my task, all tasks.

*

It is under the effect of a suicidal mood that one usually becomes infatuated by a person, an idea. What a light cast upon the essence of love and of fanaticism!

*

No greater obstacle to deliverance than the need for failure.

*

To know, in vulgar terms, is to get over something; to know, in absolute terms, is to get over everything. Illumination represents one further step: the certainty that henceforth we will never again be taken in, a last glance at illusion.

*

I strive to conceive the cosmos without . . . myself. Fortunately death is here to remedy my imagination's inadequacy.

*

Since our defects are not surface accidents but the very basis of our nature, we cannot correct them without deforming that nature, without perverting it still more.

*

What dates most is rebellion — that is, the most *vital* of our reactions.

*

In Marx's entire oeuvre, I don't think there is a single *disinterested* reflection on death. . . . I was pondering this at his grave in Highgate.

*

I'd rather offer my life as a sacrifice than be *necessary* to anything.

*

In Vedic mythology, anyone raising himself by knowledge upsets the comfort of Heaven. The gods, ever watchful, live in terror of being outclassed. Did the Boss of Genesis behave any differently? Did he not spy on man because he feared him? Because he saw him as a rival? Under these conditions, one understands the great mystics' desire to flee God, His limits and His woes, in order to seek boundlessness in the Godhead.

*

By dying, one becomes the despot of the world.

*

When you get over an infatuation, to fall for someone ever again seems so inconceivable that you imagine no one, not even a bug, that is not mired in disappointment.

*

My mission is to see things as they are. Exactly the contrary of a mission.

*

Coming from a country where failure constituted an obligation and where "I couldn't fulfill myself" was the leitmotif of all confidences . . .

*

No fate to which I could have adjusted myself. I was made to exist before my birth and after my death, not during my very existence.

*

Those nights when you convince yourself that everyone has evacuated this universe, even the dead, and that you are the last living being here, the last ghost.

*

In order to reach compassion, you must carry self-concern to the saturation point, to nausea, such paroxysms of disgust being a symptom of health, a necessary condition for looking beyond one's own trials and tribulations.

*

The true? Nowhere; everywhere effigies, from which nothing is to be expected. So why add to an initial disappointment all those that follow and that confirm it with diabolic regularity, day after day?

*

"The Holy Ghost," Luther instructs us, "is not a skeptic." Not everyone can be — and that is really too bad.

*

Discouragement, ever at the service of knowledge, hides the other side, the inner shadow, of persons and things — hence the sensation of infallibility it gives.

*

The pure passing of time, naked time, reduced to an essence of flux, without the discontinuity of the moments, is realized in our sleepless nights. Everything vanishes. Silence invades — everywhere. We listen; we hear nothing. The senses no longer turn toward the world outside. What outside? Engulfment survived by that pure passage through us that *is* ourselves, and that will come to an end only with sleep or daylight. . . .

*

Seriousness is not involved in the definition of existence; tragedy is, since it implies a notion of risk, of gratuitous disaster, whereas what is serious postulates a goal. Now, the great originality of existence is to have nothing to do with such a thing.

*

When you love someone, you hope — the more closely to be attached — that a catastrophe will strike your beloved.

*

No longer to be tempted save by what lies beyond . . .
extremes.

*

If I were to obey my first impulse, I should spend my
days writing letters of insult and adieu.

*

There is a certain shamelessness in dying. Indeed, there
is something indecent about death. This aspect, under-
standably, is the last that comes to mind.

*

I have wasted hour after hour ruminating upon what
seemed to me eminently worthy of being explored — upon
the vanity of all things, upon what does not deserve a
second's reflection, since one does not see what there is
still to be said for or against what is obvious.

*

If I prefer women to men, it is because they have the
advantage of being more off balance, hence more complex, more perspicacious, and more cynical — not to mention that mysterious superiority conferred by an age-old
slavery.

*

Akhmatova, like Gogol, wanted to possess nothing. She
gave away the presents given to her, and a few days later
they would be found in other people's houses. This characteristic recalls the behavior of nomads, compelled to the
provisional by necessity and by choice. Joseph de Maistre
cites the case of a Russian prince and his friends who
would sleep anywhere in his palace and had, so to speak,
no *fixed* bed, for they lived with the sentiment of being
transitory there, of camping out until it was time to pull up
stakes. . . . When eastern Europe furnishes such models
of detachment, why seek them out in India or elsewhere?

*

Letters one receives filled with nothing but internal debate, metaphysical interrogations, rapidly become tiresome. In everything there must be something *petty* if there is to be the impression of truth. If the angels were to write, they would be — except for the fallen ones — unreadable. *Purity* passes with difficulty because it is incompatible with breathing.

*

Out in the street, suddenly overcome by the "mystery" of Time, I told myself that Saint Augustine was quite right to deal with such a theme by addressing himself directly to God: with whom else to discuss it?

*

Everything that disturbs me I could have translated, had I been spared the shame of not being a musician.

*

A victim of crucial preoccupations, I had taken to my bed in the middle of the afternoon, an ideal position from which to ponder a nirvana *without remainder,* without the slightest trace of an ego, that obstacle to deliverance, to the state of non-thought. A sentiment of blessed extinction initially, then a blessed extinction without sentiment. I believed myself on the threshold of the final stage; it was only its parody, only the swerve into torpor, into the abyss of . . . a nap.

*

According to Jewish tradition, the Torah — God's work — preceded the world by two thousand years. Never has a people esteemed itself so highly. To attribute such priority to its sacred book, to believe it predates the *Fiat Lux*! Thus is created a destiny.

*

Having opened an anthology of religious texts, I came straight off upon this remark of the Buddha: "No object is worth being desired." I closed the book at once, for after that, what else is there to read?

*

The older we grow, the more we lack character. Each time we manage to "have" such a thing, we are uncomfortable, we feel inauthentic — whence our uneasiness in the presence of those who *smell* of conviction.

*

The felicity of having frequented a Gascon, an authentic Gascon. The particular Gascon I am thinking of, I have never seen depressed. All his disasters — and they were considerable — he described to me as triumphs. The gap between him and Don Quixote was infinitesimal. Yet he tried, my Gascon, to see clearly from time to time, though his efforts came to nothing. He remained to the end a trifler in disappointment.

*

Had I listened to my impulses, I should be, today, unhinged or hanged.

*

I have noticed that following any internal shock, my reflections, after a brief flight, take a lamentable and even grotesque turn. This has been invariably the case in my crises, whether decisive or not. As soon as one makes any sort of leap outside of life, life takes its revenge and brings one down to its level.

*

Impossible for me to know whether or not I take myself seriously. The drama of detachment is that we cannot measure its progress. We advance into a desert, and we never know where we are in it.

*

I had gone far in search of the sun, and the sun, found at last, was hostile to me. And if I were to fling myself off a cliff? While I was making such rather grim speculations, considering these pines, these rocks, these waves, I suddenly felt how bound I was to this lovely, accursed universe.

*

Quite unjustly, we grant depression only a minor status, well below that of anguish. Actually it is the more virulent affliction, but refractory to the manifestations it affects. More modest and yet more devastating, it can appear at any moment, whereas anguish, being remote, reserves itself for great occasions.

*

He comes as a tourist, and I always encounter him by chance. This time, being especially expansive, he confides to me that he is wonderfully healthy, that he is conscious of a sense of well-being at all times. I reply that his health seems suspect to me, that it is not normal to feel in continual possession of health, that true health is never *felt*. Watch out for your well-being, were my last words when I left him. Unnecessary to add that I have not encountered him since.

*

At the slightest vexation and, a fortiori, at the slightest affliction, hurry to the nearest cemetery, sudden distributor of a peace to be sought elsewhere in vain. A miracle cure, for once.

*

Regret, that backward transmigration, by resuscitating our life at will, gives us the illusion of having lived several times.

*

My weakness for Talleyrand . . . when one has practiced cynicism exclusively in words, one is filled with admiration for someone who has so magisterially translated it into action.

*

If a government decreed in midsummer that vacations were to be indefinitely extended and that, on pain of death, no one was to leave the paradise in which he was sojourning, mass suicides would follow, and unprecedented carnage.

*

Happiness and misery make me equally wretched. Then why does it sometimes happen that I prefer the former?

*

The depth of a passion is measured by the low feelings it involves — feelings that guarantee its intensity and its continuance.

*

Grim Death, a "poor portraitist," according to Goethe, gives faces something false, something outside of truth; it is assuredly not Goethe who, like Novalis, would identify death with the principle that "romanticizes" life. It must be said in his defense that having lived fifty years longer than the author of *Hymnen an die Nacht,* Goethe possessed all the time required to lose his illusions about death.

*

In the train, a middle-aged woman of a certain distinction; beside her, an idiot of thirty, her son, who occasionally took her arm and kissed it, then stared at her blissfully. She was radiant, and smiled back. What a *petrified* curiosity might be, I did not know. I know now, because I experienced it in the presence of this spectacle. A new variety of consternation was revealed to me.

*

Music exists only so long as hearing it lasts, just as God exists only so long as ecstasy lasts. The supreme art and the Supreme Being have this in common, that they depend entirely on ourselves.

*

For some — indeed, for the majority — music is stimulating and consoling. For others it is a longed-for dissolving agent, an unhoped-for means of losing themselves, of melting into what may be the best of themselves.

*

To break with one's gods, with one's ancestors, with one's language and one's country, to break *tout court,* is a terrible ordeal, that is certain; but it is also an exalting one, avidly sought by the defector and, even more, by the traitor.

*

Of all that makes us suffer, nothing — so much as disappointment — gives us the sensation of at last touching Truth.

*

As soon as one begins to "fail," instead of being upset about it, one should invoke the right of no longer being oneself.

*

We obtain almost everything, except what we secretly crave. No doubt it is fair that what we most desire should be unattainable, that the essential of ourselves and of our course through life should remain hidden and unrealized. Providence has managed things well; let each of us derive the pride and the prestige linked to intimate debacles.

*

Remaining consistent: to this end, according to the Zohar, God created man and recommended frequentation of the Tree of Life. Man, however, preferred the other tree, located in the "region of variations." His fall? A craving for change, fruit of curiosity, that source of all misfortunes. Thus what was only a whim in the first among us was to become *law* for us all.

*

A touch of pity enters into any form of attachment, into love and even into friendship, though not into admiration.

*

To leave life unscathed — this could happen but doubtless never does.

*

A too-recent disaster has the disadvantage of keeping us from perceiving its good sides.

*

Schopenhauer and Nietzsche, in the last century, spoke best of love and of music. Yet each frequented only brothels and — of all composers — the former adored Rossini, the latter Bizet.

*

Happening to encounter L., I remarked that the rivalry among the saints was the sharpest, and the most secret, of all. He asked me for examples; I found none at the moment, and find no more now. Nonetheless the fact seems to me established. . . .

*

Consciousness: summa of our discomforts from birth to the present. Such discomforts have vanished; consciousness remains — but it has lost its origins, it doesn't even know what they were.

*

Melancholy feeds on itself, and that is why it cannot renew itself.

*

In the Talmud, a stupefying assertion: "The more men

there are, the more images of the divine there are in nature." This may have been true in the period when the remark was made, but it is belied today by all one sees and will be still further belied by all that will be seen.

*

I anticipated witnessing in my lifetime the disappearance of our species. But the gods have been against me.

*

I am happy only when I contemplate renunciation and prepare myself for it. The rest is bitterness and agitation. To renounce is no easy thing, yet nothing but striving for it affords some peace. Striving? Merely thinking of it suffices to give me the illusion of being someone else, and this illusion is a victory — the most flattering one, and also the most fallacious.

*

No one had to the same degree as he a sense of the world's absurdity. Each time I alluded to it, he would utter, with a smile of complicity, the Sanskrit word *lila* — absolute gratuitousness, according to the Vedanta, the creation of the world by divine caprice. How we laughed at everything together! And now, he — the most jovial of the disabused — here he is, cast into this slough by his own fault, since he has deigned, for once, to take nothingness seriously.

6

Beckett
Some Meetings

✳

To FATHOM THIS *separate* man, we should focus on
the phrase "to hold oneself apart," the tacit motto of his
every moment, on its implication of solitude and subterranean stubbornness, on the essence of a withdrawn
being who pursues an endless and implacable labor. In
Buddhism, it is said of an adept seeking illumination that
he must be as relentless as "a mouse gnawing on a coffin."
Every authentic writer makes a similar effort. He is a de-
stroyer who *adds* to existence — who enriches by undermining it.

"Our time on earth is not long enough to spend on
anything but ourselves": this remark by a poet applies to
whoever refuses the extrinsic, the accidental, the *other*.
Beckett, or the incomparable art of being oneself. Withal,
no apparent pride, no inherent stigma, in the consciousness of being unique: if the word *amenity* did not exist, it
would have had to be invented for him. Scarcely credible,
indeed monstrous: he disparages no one, unaware of the
hygienic function of malevolence, its salutary virtues, its
executory quality. I have never heard him speak ill of

friends or enemies, a form of superiority for which I pity him and from which, unconsciously, he must suffer. If denigration were denied me, what difficulties and discomforts, what complications would result!

He lives not in time but parallel to it, which is why it has never occurred to me to ask him what he thinks of events. He is one of those beings who make you realize that history is a dimension man could have done without.

Were he like his heroes — in other words, had he gained no acceptance — he would be exactly the same. He gives the impression of not wanting to assert himself at all, of being equally alien to the notion of success and to the notion of failure. "How hard it is to figure him out! And what style he has!" I tell myself each time I think of him. If by some impossibility he concealed no secret, I would still regard him as Impenetrable.

I come from a corner of Europe where outbursts of abuse, loose talk, avowals — immediate, unsolicited, shameless disclosures — are de rigueur, where you know everything about everyone, where life in common comes down to a public confessional, and specifically where secrecy is inconceivable and volubility borders on delirium. This alone suffices to account for my fascination with a man who is supernaturally discreet.

Amenity does not exclude exasperation. At a dinner with friends, harried by absurdly pedantic questions about himself and his work, he took refuge in complete silence and actually ended by turning his back on us — or just about. The dinner was not yet over when he stood up and left, reserved and somber, as one might be before an operation or an interrogation.

*   *   *

About five years ago we ran into each other in Rue Guynemer; when he asked me if I was working, I answered that I had lost my taste for work, that I saw no need to show myself, to "produce," and that writing was a torment for me. . . . He seemed amazed by this, and I was even more amazed when, precisely with regard to writing, he spoke of *joy.* Did he actually use that word? Yes, I'm sure of it. At the same moment, I recalled that at our very first meeting, ten years earlier, at the Closerie des Lilas, he had acknowledged his great lassitude, his sense that there was nothing more to be had from words.

. . . Words: who has loved them as much as he? They are his companions, and his sole support. The man relies on no certainty, yet you feel that among them he stands fast. His fits of discouragement doubtless coincide with the moments when he stops believing in them, when he imagines they are betraying him, escaping him. Once they are gone, he remains helpless; he is nowhere. I regret not having noted and listed all the places where he refers to words, where he inclines toward them — "drops of silence through silence," as they are called in *The Unnameable.* Symbols of fragility transformed into indestructible foundations.

In English the French text *Sans* is called *Lessness,* a word coined by Beckett, as he coined the German equivalent *Losigkeit.*

This word *lessness* (as unfathomable as Boehme's *Ungrund*) so fascinated me that one evening I told him I would not sleep until I found an honorable French equivalent. . . . We considered together every possible form suggested by *sans* and *moindre.* None seemed to come close to the inexhaustible *lessness,* a mixture of privation and infinity, a vacuity synonymous with apotheosis. We parted rather disappointed. Back home, I went on

worrying about that poor *sans*. Just when I was about to
capitulate, it occurred to me that I should try something
in the direction of the Latin *sine*. I wrote him the next day
that *sinéité* seemed to me the word we were looking for.
He wrote back that he had thought of it too, perhaps at
the same moment. Yet it had to be admitted that our discovery was nothing of the kind; we agreed that the search
would have to be abandoned, that there was no French
substantive capable of expressing absence in itself, absence
in the pure state, and that we would have to resign ourselves to the metaphysical poverty of a preposition.

With writers who have nothing to say, who have no
world of their own, what can you talk about but literature? With him very rarely, in fact almost never. Everyday
subjects (material difficulties, problems of all kinds) interest him more — in conversation, of course. What he cannot endure in any case is questions like Do you think that
such-and-such a work will last? Does so-and-so deserve
the rank he has? Between X and Y, who will survive, who
is the greater figure? Any evaluation of this kind exasperates and depresses him. "What's the sense in all that!" he
exclaimed to me after one particularly painful evening
when the dinner-table conversation resembled a grotesque
version of the Last Judgment. He himself avoids com-
menting on his books, his plays: what matters to him is
not the obstacles surmounted but those to be surmounted:
he identifies himself totally with what he is doing. If you
ask him about a play, he will discuss not the content, the
meaning, but the interpretation, whose slightest details he
envisions, minute by minute, almost second by second. I
shall not soon forget the energy with which he explained
the requirements to be satisfied by any actress who wanted

to perform *Not I,* in which only a gasping voice dominates space and replaces it. How bright his eyes when he *saw* that tiny yet encroaching, omnipresent voice! It was as if he were watching the ultimate metamorphosis, the supreme collapse of the Pythia!

Having been a cemetery buff all my life, and knowing that Beckett loved them, too (*First Love,* it will be recalled, begins with the description of a cemetery, one that happens to be in Hamburg), I spoke to him last winter, on Avenue de l'Observatoire, of a recent visit to Père-Lachaise and of my indignation at not finding Proust on the list of "notables" buried there. (Let me say in passing that the first time I came across Beckett's name was some thirty years ago, when I found his little book on Proust in the American Library.) I don't know how we came to mention Swift, although, on reflection, the transition had nothing abnormal about it, given the funereal character of his humor. Beckett told me that he was rereading *Gulliver* and that he had a predilection for the "country of the Houyhnhnms," particularly for the scene where Gulliver feels such terror and disgust at the approach of a female Yahoo. He told me — and this was a great surprise, certainly a great disappointment — that Joyce didn't like Swift. Moreover, he added, Joyce had no inclination for satire, contrary to what one might think. "He never rebelled; he was detached; he accepted everything. For him, *there was no difference between the fall of a bomb and the fall of a leaf. . . .*"

A marvelous judgment that in its acuteness and its strange density reminds me of how Armand Robin once answered a question I put to him: "Why, after translating so many poets, haven't you ever tried Chuang-tse, who has more poetry in him than all the sages?" "I've often thought of it," he replied, "but how can you translate a work that is comparable only to the *barren countryside of northern Scotland?*"

How many times, since I've known Beckett, have I wondered (an obsessive and rather stupid interrogation) about his relation to his characters. What do they share? Who could conceive of a more radical disparity? Can it be true that not only their existence but his, too, is steeped in that "leaden light" described in *Malone Dies?* More than one of his pages seems to me a sort of monologue *after* the end of some cosmic epoch. . . . The sensation of entering into a posthumous universe, some geography dreamed by a demon released from everything, even his own malediction.

Beings who do not know whether they are still alive, subject to an enormous fatigue *not of this world* (to use a language contrary to Beckett's tastes), all conceived by a man whom we guess to be vulnerable and who for decency's sake wears the mask of invulnerability — not long ago, I had a sudden vision of the links that bind them to their author, to their accomplice. What I saw then, or rather what I felt, I cannot translate into an intelligible formula; nonetheless, ever since, the merest remark of one of his heroes reminds me of the inflections of a certain voice. . . . But I hasten to add that a revelation can be as fragile and as mendacious as a theory.

Ever since our first encounter, I have realized that he reached *the limit,* that he perhaps began there, at the impossible, at the exceptional, at the impasse. And the admirable thing is that he has not *budged,* that having come up against a wall from the start, he has persevered, as valiant as he has always been: the limit-situation as point of departure, the end as advent! Which accounts for the feeling that that world of his, though always tottering on the verge of death, may continue indefinitely, whereas ours will soon disappear.

I am not especially attracted by Wittgenstein's philosophy, but I have a passion for the man himself. Everything I read about him has the gift of stirring me. More than once I have found features he and Beckett share. Two mysterious apparitions, two phenomena one is glad to find so baffling, so inscrutable. In both, the same distance from beings and things, the same inflexibility, the same temptation to silence, to the final repudiation of the word, the same will to collide with frontiers never foreseen. In other ages, they would have been lured by the Desert. We know now that Wittgenstein at a certain point actually envisaged entering a monastery. As for Beckett, how easy to imagine him, some centuries back, in a naked cell, undisturbed by the least decoration, not even a crucifix. Do I digress? Just remember that remote, enigmatic, "inhuman" gaze of his in certain photographs.

Granted, our beginnings matter, but we make the decisive step toward ourselves only when we no longer have an *origin,* when we offer as little substance for a biography as God. . . . It is both important and utterly unimportant that Beckett is Irish. What is dead wrong is to maintain (a French assertion?) that he is "the typical Anglo-Saxon." Certainly nothing would displease him more. Is it his bad memories of his prewar stay in London? I suspect him of finding the British "vulgar." This verdict that he has not passed — which I am passing for him as a shortcut to his reservations, if not his resentments — I could scarcely adopt for my own, especially because (a Balkan illusion, perhaps) the British strike me as the most devitalized and the most threatened nation, hence the most refined, the most *civilized*.

Beckett, who oddly enough feels quite at home in France, has in reality no affinity with a certain dryness, an eminently French virtue, or at least a Parisian one. Is it not significant that he versified Chamfort? Not all Chamfort, of course; only a few maxims. The enterprise, remarkable in itself and in fact almost inconceivable (if we think of the absence of lyric impulse that characterizes the moralists' skeletal prose), is equivalent to an avowal, if not a proclamation. It is always in spite of themselves that secret minds betray the depths of their nature. Beckett's is so impregnated with poetry that it is inseparable from it.

I find him as obstinate as any fanatic. Even if the world crumbled, he would not abandon the work under way, nor would he alter his subject. In the essential things, he is certainly not to be influenced. As for the rest, the inessential, he is defenseless, probably as weak as all of us, even weaker than his characters. . . . Before collecting these notes, I had intended to reread what Meister Eckhart and Nietzsche wrote, from their different perspectives, about "the noble man." I have not carried out my project, but I have not forgotten for a single moment that I had conceived it.

1976

7

Meeting the Moments

✳

It IS NOT BY GENIUS, it is by suffering, by suffering only, that one ceases to be a marionette.

✳

When we fall under the spell of death, everything occurs as if we had known death in a previous existence, and as if now we were impatient to get back to it as soon as possible.

✳

Once you suspect someone of having the slightest weakness for the Future, you can be sure he knows the address of more than one psychiatrist.

✳

"Your truths make it impossible to breathe."

"Impossible *for you*," I immediately replied to this innocent. Yet I might have wanted to add; "And for me, too," instead of swashbuckling. . . .

✳

Man is not content to be man. But he doesn't know what to revert to, nor how to recover a state of which he has no clear memory. His nostalgia for it is the basis of his being, and it is by such nostalgia he communicates with all that remains of what is oldest in himself.

*

In the deserted church, the organist was practicing. No one else there, except a cat that wreathed itself around me. . . . Its eagerness was a shock: the inveterate tormenting questions assailed me. The organ's answer did not seem satisfying to me, but in my condition, it was an answer nonetheless.

*

The ideally truthful being, whom we are always permitted to imagine, would be someone who, at any moment, would not seek refuge in euphemism.

*

Unrivaled in the worship of Impassivity, I have aspired to it frantically, so that the more I strained to achieve it, the further from it I found myself. A just defeat for a man who pursues a goal contrary to his nature.

*

Man proceeds from one chaos to the next. This consideration is of no consequence and keeps no one from fulfilling his destiny — from acceding, in short, to the *integral* chaos.

*

Anxiety, far from deriving from a nervous disequilibrium, is based on the very constitution of this world, and there is no reason why one should not be anxious at every moment, given that time itself is merely anxiety fully expanded, an anxiety whose beginning and end are indistinguishable, an eternally victorious anxiety.

*

Under an incomparably desolate sky, two birds, indifferent to that lugubrious background, pursue one another. . . . Their obvious delight is more apt to rehabilitate an old instinct than the entire body of erotic literature.

*

Tears of admiration: sole excuse for this universe, since one must be found.

*

Out of solidarity with a friend who had just died, I closed my eyes and let myself be flooded by that semi-chaos preceding sleep. After a few minutes I began to realize that infinitesimal reality which still binds us to consciousness. Was I on the threshold of the end? A second later I was at the bottom of an abyss, without the slightest trace of fear. Then was no-longer-existing so simple? Probably, if death were only an experiment; but it is The Experiment. And what a notion, to *play* with a phenomenon that occurs but once! One does not test the unique.

*

The more one has suffered, the less one demands. To protest is a sign one has traversed no hell.

*

As if I didn't have enough troubles, here I am harassed by those that must have been known to the caveman.

*

We hate ourselves because we cannot forget ourselves, because we cannot think of anything else. It is inevitable that we should be exasperated by this excessive preference and that we should struggle to triumph over it. Yet hating ourselves is the least effective stratagem by which to manage it.

*

Music is an illusion that makes up for all the others. (If *illusion* is a term doomed to disappear, I wonder what will become of me.)

*

To no one is it vouchsafed, in a state of neutrality, to perceive the pulsation of Time. To achieve this, a malaise sui generis is necessary, a favor proceeding from who knows where?

*

When we have glimpsed vacuity and offered sunyata a worship alternately patent and clandestine, we are helpless to ally ourselves with a personal, incarnated, paltry god. From another aspect, nakedness unscathed by any presence, by any human contamination, scoured of the very idea of a self, compromises the possibility of any worship whatever, necessarily linked to a whiff of individual supremacy. For as a hymn of Mahayana Buddhism has it, "if all things are empty, who is celebrated, and by whom?"

*

Much more than time, it is sleep that is the antidote to grief. Insomnia, on the other hand, which enlarges the slightest vexation and converts it into a blow of fate, stands vigil over our wounds and keeps them from flagging.

*

Instead of paying attention to the faces of people passing by, I watched their feet, and all these busy types were reduced to hurrying steps — toward what? And it was clear to me that our mission was to graze the dust in search of a mystery stripped of anything serious.

*

The first thing I was told by a friend who had dropped out of sight for many years: though he had accumulated a stock of poisons over a long period, he had not managed to kill himself because he could not decide which one to take.

*

We do not undermine our reasons for living without at the same time undermining those for *writing*.

*

Nonreality is an obvious matter I forget and rediscover every day. So intimately does this farce become part of my existence that I cannot dissociate them. Why this buffoonery of starting all over again? Yet it is no such thing, for by this means I belong among the living, or appear to do so.

*

Every individual, as such, even before actually falling, has already fallen, and to the antipodes of his original model.

*

How to explain that the fact of not having been, that the colossal absence preceding birth, seems to disturb no one, and that even the person who is troubled by it is not troubled to any excessive extent?

*

According to a Chinese sage, a single hour of happiness is all that a centenarian could acknowledge after carefully reflecting upon the vicissitudes of his existence. . . . Since everyone exaggerates, why should the sages constitute an exception?

*

I should like to forget *everything* and waken to a light *before time*.

*

Melancholy redeems this universe, and yet it is melancholy that separates us from it.

*

To have passed one's youth at a demiurgic temperature. . . .

*

How many disappointments are conducive to bitterness? One or a thousand, depending on the subject.

*

To conceive the act of thought as a poison bath, the
pastime of an elegaic viper.

*

God is the conditioned creature par excellence, the
slave of slaves, prisoner of His attributes, of what He *is*.
Man, on the contrary, has a certain leeway insofar as he
is not — insofar as, possessing only a borrowed existence,
he struggles in pseudoreality.

*

To assert itself, life gives evidence of a rare ingenuity;
and no less to deny itself. What it has invented as ways of
getting rid of itself! Death is far and away its greatest find,
its most prodigious success.

*

The clouds passed by. In the silence of the night, you
could have heard the noise they were making as they
rushed overhead. Why are we here? what meaning can our
infinitesimal presence have? Questions without answers,
though I reply spontaneously, without the shadow of reflection and without blushing at uttering such a distinguished banality: "It is in order to torment ourselves that
we are here, and for no other reason."

*

Had I been informed that my moments, like all the rest,
were going to abandon me, I should have felt neither fear,
nor regret, nor joy. Flawless absence. Every personal accent had vanished from what I thought I was still feeling,
but in truth I was feeling nothing, I was surviving my own
sensations, and yet I was not a living dead man: I was
alive, but as one is seldom alive, as one is alive only once.

＊

To frequent the Desert Fathers and yet to be moved by the latest news! In the first centuries of our era, I would have belonged among those eremites of whom it is said that after a certain time they were "wearied with seeking God."

＊

Though we ourselves have come too late, we shall be envied by our immediate successors, and still more by our remote descendants. In their eyes we shall have the look of privileged characters, and rightly so, for everyone wants to be as far as possible from the future.

＊

Let no one enter if he has spent a single day in stupor's refuge!

＊

Our place is somewhere between being and nonbeing — between two fictions.

＊

The other, it must be confessed, seems to us more or less of a lunatic. We follow him only up to a point; after that he necessarily strays, since even his most legitimate concerns strike us as unjustified, inexplicable.

＊

Never ask language to furnish an effort out of proportion to its natural capacity; in any case, do not force it to yield its maximum. Let us avoid all extravagance with words, lest, bewildered, they can no longer bear the burden of a meaning.

＊

No thought more corrosive nor more reassuring than the thought of death. Doubtless it is because of this double quality that we brood over it to the point of being unable to do without it. What luck to meet up, in one and the same moment, with a poison and a remedy, a revelation that kills yet gives life, a roborant venom!

*

After the Goldberg Variations — "superessential music," to employ the mystical jargon — we close our eyes, giving ourselves up to the echo they have raised within us. Nothing more exists, except a plenitude *without content,* which is indeed the sole way of approaching the Supreme.

*

To attain deliverance, we must believe that everything is real, or else that nothing is. But we distinguish only *degrees* of reality; things strike us as more or less true, more or less *in being.* And so it is that we never know where we are.

*

To trace back to the sovereign zero, out of which emerges that subaltern zero that constitutes ourselves. . . .

*

The Serious is not quite an attribute of existence; the Tragic is, for it implies a notion of gratuitous disaster, whereas the Serious suggests a minimum of finality. And the charm of existence is that it allows of none.

*

Each of us passes through his Promethean crisis, and all we do afterward is revel in or revile that past.

*

To exhibit a skull in a showcase: already a challenge; a whole skeleton, a scandal. After even the most furtive glance, how will the passing wretch attend to his affairs, and in what mood will the poor lover proceed to his assignation? With all the more reason, a prolonged halt before our ultimate metamorphosis can only discourage desire and delirium. . . . And thus it is that as I walked away, there was nothing for me to do but curse that vertical horror and its uninterrupted sneer.

*

"When the bird of sleep thought to nest in my pupils, it saw the lashes and fled in fear of the net." Who better than this Ben al-Hamara, an Arab poet of Andalusia, has perceived the unfathomability of insomnia?

*

Those moments when a memory or even less is enough to slip out of the world.

*

Even as a runner who stops in the heat of the race, trying to understand the meaning of it all: to meditate is an admission that one is winded.

*

Enviable form of renown: to attach our name, like our first ancestor, to mud that will dazzle the generations of men.

*

"What is impermanent is suffering; what is suffering is non-self. What is non-self is not mine; I am not that, that is not I" (*Samyutta Nikaya*). *What is suffering is non-self.* It is difficult, it is impossible, to agree with Buddhism on this point, crucial though it is. For us, suffering is what is most ourselves, most self. What a strange religion! It sees suffering everywhere yet at the same time declares it to be unreal.

*

On his countenance, not a trace of mockery remaining. It is because he had an almost sordid attachment to life. Those who have not deigned to cling to it wear a scornful smile, sign of deliverance and of triumph. They are not going into nothingness; they have left it behind.

＊

Before his serious health problems, he was a scholar; since . . . he has *fallen* into metaphysics. To be accessible to that essential divagation, the cooperation of loyal miseries is necessary — those eager to recur.

＊

To have borne the Himalayas all night long — and to call that *sleep*.

＊

What sacrifice would I not make in order to be free of this wretched self, which at this very moment occupies, within the All, a place no god has dared aspire to!

＊

It takes an enormous humility to die. The strange thing is that everyone turns out to have it!

＊

These waves and their sempiternal prattle are eclipsed, in futility, by the yet more inept trepidation of the city. If you close your eyes and let yourself sink beneath this double rumbling, you imagine yourself present at the sketches for the Creation, and you rapidly lose your way in cosmogonic lucubrations. Wonder of wonders: no interval between the first agitation and this unnameable point we have reached.

＊

Every form of *progress* is a perversion, in the sense that *being* is a perversion of nonbeing.

＊

You may have endured insomnias of which a martyr would be jealous, but if they have not marked your features, no one will believe you. Without witnesses, you will continue to seem some kind of joker, and acting the part better than anyone, you yourself will be the first accomplice of the incredulous.

*

Proof that a generous action goes against nature: it provokes — sometimes immediately, sometimes months or years later — an uneasiness one dares not admit to anyone, even to oneself.

*

At that funeral service, everything was *shadow* and *dream* and dust returning to dust. Then, without transition, the deceased was promised eternal joy and all that follows from it. So much inconsistency vexed me, and I forsook both the Greek Orthodox pope and the late-lamented. As I left, I could not help thinking that I was in no position to protest against those who so ostensibly contradict themselves.

*

What a relief to throw into the garbage a manuscript, witness of a fallen fever, of a disconcerting frenzy!

*

This morning I *thought*, hence lost my bearings, for a good quarter of an hour.

*

Everything that inconveniences us allows us to define ourselves. Without indispositions, no identity — the luck and misfortune of a *conscious* organism.

*

If to describe a misery were as easy as to live through it!

*

Daily lesson in reserve: to realize, if only for the wink of an eye, that one day people will speak of our *remains*.

*

People insist on the *diseases* of the will; they forget that the will as such is suspect, and that it is not *normal* to will.

*

After having palavered for hours, I am invaded by the void. By the void and by shame. Is it not indecent to display one's secrets, to proffer one's very being, to tell and to tell *oneself,* whereas the fullest moments of one's life have been known in silence, in the *perception* of silence?

*

As an adolescent, Turgenev tacked to his bedroom wall a portrait of Fouquier-Tinville. Youth, always and everywhere, has idealized executioners, provided they perform their task in the name of the vague and the bombastic.

*

Life and death have little enough content, the one as well as the other. Unfortunately we always know this too late, when it can no longer help us either to live or to die.

*

You are calm, you forget your enemy, who meanwhile watches and waits. Yet there is every reason to be ready when he attacks. You will triumph, for he will be weakened by that enormous consumption of energy, his hatred.

*

Of all things one feels, nothing gives the impression of being at the very heart of truth so much as fits of *unaccountable* despair; compared to these, everything seems frivolous, debased, lacking in substance and interest.

*

Weariness independent of the organs' wear and tear, timeless weariness, for which no palliative exists, and over which no rest, even the last, can triumph. . . .

*

Everything is salutary, save to question ourselves moment by moment as to the meaning of our actions: everything is preferable to the only question that matters.

*

Having once been concerned with Joseph de Maistre, instead of explaining the figure by accumulating details, I should have recalled that he managed to sleep only three hours a night, at the most. This suffices to account for the extravagances of a thinker, or of anyone at all. Yet I had neglected to observe the phenomenon — an all the more unforgivable omission in that human beings are divided into *sleepers* and *wakers,* two specimens of beings, forever heterogeneous, with nothing but their physical aspect in common.

*

We should really breathe better if one fine day we were told that the quasi-totality of our kind had evaporated as if by magic.

*

You must have powerful religious dispositions in order to utter with conviction the word *being;* you must *believe* simply to say about an object or about someone that it or he *is.*

*

Every season is an ordeal; nature changes and renews herself only in order to *scourge* us.

*

At the source of the least thought appears a slight disequilibrium. What then are we to say about the kind from which thought itself proceeds?

*

If in "primitive" societies the old are disposed of a little too readily, in "civilized" ones, on the other hand, they are flattered and overfed. The future, no doubt about it, will retain only the first model.

*

Though you abandon all religious or political faith, you will preserve the tenacity and the intolerance that impelled you to adopt it. You will still be in a rage, but your rage will be directed *against* the abandoned belief; fanaticism, linked to your very essence, will persist there independent of the convictions you can defend or reject. The basis, your basis, remains the same, and it is not by changing opinions that you will manage to modify it.

*

The Zohar puts us in a quandary: if it is telling the truth, the poor man presents himself before God with only his soul, while the others have nothing to offer but their bodies. Given the impossibility of making a choice, best to keep on waiting.

*

Do not confuse talent and verve. Most often verve will characterize the charlatan. From another point of view, without it, how give any spice to our truths, to our errors?

*

Not a moment when I am not incredulous at finding myself in just that moment.

*

Out of dozens of our dreams, only one has any meaning, and even then! The rest — discards, simplistic or vomitive literature, imagery of sickly genius. The dreams that are long-drawn-out testify to the indigence of the "dreamer," who cannot see how to conclude and struggles unsuccessfully to find a *dénouement,* just as in the theater the playwright multiplies peripeties, not knowing how and where to stop.

*

My problems — or rather, my pains — follow a policy that is beyond me. Sometimes they are concerted and advance together, sometimes each goes its own way, very often they oppose each other, but whether they agree or dispute, they behave as if their maneuvers had nothing to do with me, as if I were merely their flabbergasted spectator.

*

Only what we have not accomplished and what we could not accomplish matters to us, so that what remains of a whole life is only what it will not have been.

*

To dream of an enterprise of demolition that would spare none of the traces of the original Big Bang.

8

Saint-John Perse

✳

Bᴜᴛ ᴡʜᴀᴛ ɪs ᴛʜɪs, oh! what is it, in each thing, that suddenly falls short?" No sooner is the question asked than the poet, dismayed by the evident sources from which it rises (as though from the abyss to which it leads), turns against it and wages — in order to compromise it, to destroy its insidious authority — a battle whose details and vicissitudes we do not know, as we do not know what secrets this abstract confidence conceals: "There is no history save of the soul." Reluctant to divulge his history, he condemns us to guess or to construct it, hides behind the very avowals to which he assents, and does not intend us to touch the "pure keys" of his exile. Impenetrable out of a certain modesty, anything but inclined to the abdications of limpidity, the compromises of transparency, he has multiplied his masks, and if he has enlarged himself beyond the immediate and the finite, past that intelligibility which is limit and acquiescence to limit, it is not in order to espouse the Vague, poetic prelude to vacuity, but to "haunt Being," his sole means of escaping the terror of insolvency, the flashing perception of what, in each thing, "falls short." Rarely given, almost always conquered, Being well deserves the honor of a capital letter; in this case the conquest is so brilliant that it seems to emanate from a revelation rather than from a process or a struggle — whence the frequent surprises, the sensation of the instantaneous. "And suddenly everything is power and presence for me, there where the theme of nothingness is smoking still"; "The sea itself, like a sudden ovation . . ." Aside from the abyssal interrogation quoted above, emphasis is laid on the sudden, on the unforeseen, so as to mark the emergence and the sovereignty of the positive, the transfiguration of the inanimate, victory over the void.

To have celebrated Exile, to have replaced the *I* as much as possible by *the Stranger,* yet to come to terms with the world, to find anchorage there, to become its spokesman — such is the paradox of a continually triumphant lyricism in which each word inclines toward the thing it translates, so as to bring it level with an apparently undeserved order, so as to hoist it up to the miracle of a never-vanquished Yes and to enfold it in a hymn to diversity, to the iridescent image of the One. An erudite and virgin lyricism, concerted and original, produced from a knowledge of life-fluids, from a learned intoxication with the elements, pre-Socratic and antibiblical, a lyricism that calls sacred everything capable of bearing a name, everything over which language — that true savior — can have a hold. To justify things is to baptize them, is to wrest them from their darkness, their anonymity; insofar as he succeeds, he will love them all, even that "golgotha of ordure and rust," the modern city. (The recourse — however ironic — to Christian terminology has a strange effect in a fundamentally pagan work.)

At once emanation and exegesis of a demiurge, the

Poem — which, in Perse's vision, proceeds as much from cosmogony as from literature — is elaborated like a universe: it engenders, enumerates, compares the elements, and incorporates them into its nature. The Poem is closed, subsisting in and of itself, yet open ("a whole mute nation rises in my words"), restive yet subjugated, autonomous yet dependent, as attached to expression as it is to the expressed, to the subject that savors itself and to the subject that records: the poem is ecstasy and enumeration, inventory and absolute. Sometimes, merely responding to its formal aspects and forgetting that it sounds reality, we are tempted to read it as if it were no more than the glamour of its music, as if it corresponded to nothing objective, nothing perceptible. "Beautiful, all right — like Sanskrit!" our passive and enchanted ego exclaims, capitulating to the voluptuous delights of language as such. But this language, once again, adheres to the object and reflects its appearances. The space it delights in is that "*Raum der Rühmung*" dear to Rilke, that space of celebration in which reality, never unfulfilled, tends toward a surplus of being, in which each thing participates in the Supreme because nothing falls under the curse of the Interchangeable, source of negation and cynicism.

Existence is legitimate and valuable only if we are capable of discerning, at whatever level, even that of the infinitesimal, the presence of the irreplaceable. If we fail, we reduce the spectacle of process to a series of equivalences and simulacra, to a play of appearances against a background of identity. We imagine ourselves clearsighted, and doubtless we are, but our perspicacity, by dint of making us waver between the futile and the funereal, ends by plunging us into fruitless ruminations, in the abuse of irony and the complacencies of denial. Despair-

ing of ever being able to confer upon our imprecise ani-
mosities the density of venom, and, moreover, weary of
laboring over the invalidation of Being, we turn to those
who, engaged in the enterprise of praise, superior to the
shadows, exempt from the superstition of negation, dare
consent to everything, because for them everything counts,
everything is irreparably unique. The Poem will celebrate,
precisely, uniqueness — not that of the passing moment,
an inconsequence, but the uniqueness in which the eternal
exception of each thing is deployed. In that epoch of celebration, there is only one dimension: the present — limitless duration that enfolds the ages, a moment at once
immemorial and actual. Are we in this age? Or at the
dawn of Greece or China? Nothing more illegitimate than
to bring chronological scruples to a work and an author
blessedly unscathed by them. Like the Poem, Perse is a
contemporary — a timeless one.

> "I shall be there among the very first for the irruption of
> the new god."

We feel, ourselves, that he has already witnessed both advent and twilight of the old gods, and that if he anticipates
others, he does so not as a prophet but as a mind in which
reminiscence and presentiment, far from taking opposite
paths, unite and coincide. Closer to oracle than to dogma
(an initiate by energy and attitude, by what we might call
his Delphic aspect), he espouses no specific cult: how condescend to the god of others, how share him with them?
For all that he idolizes words, converting their fiction into
essence, the poet creates a private mythology, his own
Olympus, which he populates and depopulates at will, a
privilege he is granted by language, whose proper role and
final function is to engender and destroy the gods.

No more than he affects any specific period, the Stranger of the Poem takes root in no country. He seems to traverse some empire celebrating an inexhaustible festivity. The human beings he encounters there and their customs doubtless attract him, though less than the elements. Even in books he will seek the wind and the "thought of the wind," and more than the wind, the sea, invested with the attributes and advantages ordinarily enjoyed by divinity: "unity restored," "light made substance for us," "Being surprised in its essence," "luminous instance." . . . In its infinite productivity (in many respects, does it not evoke the Night of the romantics?), the sea will be an Absolute arrayed, a fathomless wonder yet a visible one, revelation of a bottomless appearance. The Poem will have as its mission to imitate the sea's undulation and brilliance, to suggest its perfection in incompletion, to be or to seem a swirling eternity, coexistence of the past and the possible within a Becoming without succession, a duration that endlessly falls back upon itself.

Neither historical nor tragic, Perse's vision, emancipated from both terror and nostalgia, partakes of the Tremor, of that tonic shudder of a mind that has "built upon the abyss" instead of falling into it and cultivating its pangs. No predilection here for panic, but the ecstasy that triumphs over vacuity, the sensuality of awe. From his universe (in which the flesh acquires a metaphysical status), evil is banished, and good as well, for here existence finds its justification in itself. Truly? When the poet has doubts, when he cannot sound Being as he might the sea, then he turns to language in order to study its "great erosions," to explore its depths, the "old layers." Immersion complete, he surfaces again to utter, like the waves, "one long unstopped sentence forever unintelligible."

Were a single meaning to be attached to work, it would be condemned without appeal; stripped of that halo of indeterminacy and ambiguity which flatters and multiplies its commentators, it collapses in the woes of clarity and, ceasing to dismay, suffers the dishonor reserved for the obvious. If the work would avoid the humiliation of being understood, it must, by a certain dosage of the unimpeachable and the obscure, by attention to the equivocal, provoke divergent interpretations and perplexed fervors, those symptoms of vitality, those guarantees of *lasting*. It is lost once it permits the commentator to know at what level of reality it is located and of what world it is the reflection. The author, no less than the work, must dissimulate his identity, yield everything of himself except the essential, persevere in his enchantment and his solitude, a sovereign subservient to his words, their dazzled slave. Even so evident a master of words as Perse, we cannot help feeling, suffers their despotism, which in his fascination he identifies with the elements, even with the elemental — with the caprices and commands from which he can never escape.

This impression may be corrected by another, contrary one, every bit as legitimate: the more we read him, the more we discern in Perse the dimension of a legislator impatient to codify the vague and the impalpable, to call words to order . . . , to wrest them from their anarchy or rouse them from their torpor, in order to send them to our aid, charged with salubrious and vivifying truths. Antithetical to a Valéry or an Eliot ("Ash Wednesday" is the exact antipodes of the world of Perse), he avoids insisting on the "purity of Nonbeing" or on the "infirm glory of the positive hour," and when he invokes death, it is to denounce its "immense pomps," not to exploit its magic. A poet in his complicity, his affinity, with beings and with things, he neither regrets nor condemns that original rupture which swept them out of unity, into a procession — anything but funereal, according to him, actually blessed, since it provoked that parade of the multiple, of the patent and the strange, whose exhaustive accounting he undertakes. Everything one sees deserves to be seen, whatever exists is incurably *existent,* he seems to be telling us, while, in a trance, in the vertigo of plenitude, in an orgiastic appetite for reality, he labors to fill, to cram, the void, without inflicting upon it that scourge of opacity and gravitation which discredits matter.

There are poets whose help we seek in our will-to-wane; we want them to encourage our gainsaying, to aggravate our stupor, our vice. They are irresistible, marvelously debilitating. . . . There are other poets, more difficult of access because they do not espouse our rancors and our obsessions. Mediators in the conflict that sets us against the world, they invite us to acceptance, to an effort over the ego. . . . When we are overcome by ourselves, and still more by our cries, when that eminently modern craving to protest and to assert our rights assumes the gravity of a sin, what a comfort to encounter a mind that never falls into such ways, that retreats from the vulgarity of revolt, like a man of antiquity, of both heroic antiquity and waning antiquity, like Pindar or even like Marcus Aurelius, who exclaimed, "Whatever the hours bring me is a flavorsome fruit, O Nature." In Perse there is a note of lyric *sagesse,* a superb litany of contentment, an apotheosis of necessity and expression, of fate and of the word, just as there is, without the slightest Christian accent, a visionary side. "And the star of no nation climbs into the heights of the green age": do we not seem to be reading some verses of a *serene* variant of the Apocalypse? Were the universe to vanish, nothing would be lost, since language would immediately take its place. If just one word, a simple word, were to survive the general engulfment, it would in itself defy nothingness. Such is the conclusion the Poem implies and demands.

1960

9

Exasperations

*

AT TWO in the afternoon, rowing on the Étang de, Soustons, I was suddenly thunderstruck by the recollection of a phrase: *All is of no avail.* Had I been alone, I should have flung myself into the water then and there. Never have I felt with such violence the necessity of putting an end to it all.

*

Devouring biographies one after the next to be convinced of the futility of any undertaking, of any destiny.

*

I run into X. I would have given anything in the world never to encounter him again. To have to endure such specimens! While he talked, I was inconsolable not to possess a supernatural power that could annihilate both of us on the spot.

*

This body — what use is it, if not to make us understand the meaning of the word *torturer*?

*

An acute sense of absurdity makes the merest action

unlikely, indeed impossible. Lucky those who lack such a thing! Providence has looked out for them.

*

At an exhibit of Oriental art, a many-headed Brahma, irritated, sullen, besotted to the last degree. It is in this attitude that I enjoy seeing representations of the god of gods.

*

Out of patience with them all. But I like to laugh. And I cannot laugh alone.

*

Never having known what I was after in this world, I am still waiting for someone to tell me what he himself pursues.

*

Asked why the monks who followed him were so . . . radiant, Buddha answered that it was because they thought neither of the past nor of the future. We turn gloomy, in fact, whenever we contemplate either one, and worse than gloomy whenever we contemplate both.

*

Counterirritant to desolation: close your eyes for a long while in order to forget light and all that it reveals.

*

When a writer passes himself off as a philosopher, you can be sure he does so in order to camouflage any number of deficiencies. Ideas: a screen that hides nothing.

*

In admiration as in envy, the eyes suddenly light up. How to distinguish one from the other in those we are uncertain about?

*

He calls me in the middle of the night to tell me he

can't sleep. I give him a good lecture on this variety of disaster, which is, in reality, disaster itself. At the end I am so pleased with my performance that I go back to bed feeling like a hero, proud to confront the hours separating me from daylight.

*

The publication of a book involves the same kinds of problems as a marriage or a funeral.

*

Never write about anyone. I am so convinced of this that each time I am inclined to do so, my first thought is to attack, *even if I admire him,* the person of whom I am to speak.

*

"And God saw that the light was good": such is the opinion of mortals, with the exception of the sleepless, for whom it is an aggression, a new inferno more pitiless than the night's.

*

There comes a moment when negation itself loses its luster and, much deteriorated, goes down the drain with appearances.

*

According to Louis de Broglie, there is a relation between "*faire de l'esprit*" and making scientific discoveries, *esprit* here signifying the capacity "spontaneously to establish unexpected comparisons." If this were so, the Germans would be incapable of innovating with regard to the sciences. Swift himself was amazed that a nation of dullards should have so great a number of inventions to its credit; but invention does not suppose agility so much as perseverance — the capacity to explore, to penetrate, to persist. . . . The spark is struck by obstinacy.

Nothing is tiresome for a man swept on by the craving for investigation. Proof against boredom, he will expatiate endlessly about anything, without sparing, if he is a writer, his readers; without even deigning, if he is a philosopher, to take them into consideration.

*

I tell an American psychoanalyst that while on a friend's property, I happened to take a bad fall while I was doing some of my inveterate pruning, struggling with the dry branches of a sequoia. "You were 'struggling' with that tree not to prune it, but to punish it for outliving you. Your secret desire was to take revenge by stripping it of its branches." Enough to disgust one forever with any *deep* explanation.

*

Another Yankee, this time a professor, was complaining that he didn't know what he would discuss in his next year's lectures.

"Why not chaos and its charms?"

"I don't know about that — I've never been subject to that kind of spell," he replied. Easier to reach an understanding with a monster than with the contrary of a monster.

*

I was reading Rimbaud — *Le Bateau ivre* — to someone who didn't know the poem and who, moreover, was a stranger to poetry itself. "It sounds as if it came from the tertiary age" was his comment, once I had finished reading. As judgments go, not bad.

*

P. Tz.: a genius if ever there was one. Oral frenzy, out of a horror or an impossibility of writing. Scattered through the Balkans, thousands and thousands of quips, lost forever. How to give a notion of his verve, his passion, his madness? "You're a mixture of God and Quixote," I told him once. At the time he was flattered, but the next morning, very early, he came to tell me, "I don't like that business about Don Quixote."

*

From the age of ten to the age of fourteen, I lived in a boardinghouse. Every morning on my way to school, passing a bookstore, I would glance at the books, which were changed relatively often, even in this provincial Rumanian town. Only one, in the corner of the shop window, seemed to have been forgotten for months: *Bestia umana* (Zola's *Human Beast*). Of those four years, the only memory that haunts me is that title.

*

My books, *my* work: the grotesquerie of such possessives. Everything was spoiled once literature stopped being anonymous. Decadence dates from the first *author*.

*

I had decided never again to shake hands with anyone healthy. Yet I have had to compromise, for I soon discovered that many of those I suspected of well-being were less subject to it than I had supposed. What was the use of making enemies on the basis of mere suspicions?

*

Nothing so hampers continuity of thought as to feel the mind's insistent pressure. Perhaps this is why the mad think only in *flashes*.

*

That man in the street — what does he want? Why is he alive? And that child and its mother, and that old man? No one finds favor in my eyes during this accursed promenade. At last I went into a butcher shop, where something like half a calf's carcass was hanging. At the sight I was quite ready to burst into tears.

＊

In my fits of rage I feel vexatiously close to Saint Paul. My affinities with the frantic — with all whom I detest . . . who has ever so resembled his antipodes?

＊

Looming up out of a sort of primordial Ineffectuality. . . . Just now, trying to contend with a serious subject and failing altogether, I went to bed. How frequently have my plans led me to this predestined term of all my ambitions!

＊

There is always someone above you: beyond God Himself *rises* Nothingness.

＊

To perish! — that verb which is my favorite and which, oddly enough, suggests nothing irreparable.

＊

Whenever I have to meet someone, I am overcome with such a craving for isolation that when I am about to speak, I lose all control over my words, and their somersaulting is taken for . . . verve!

＊

This universe, so magisterially miscarried — as one keeps telling onself when one happens to be in a concessive mood.

＊

Braggadocio and physical pain do not go together. As soon as our carcass makes itself known, we are brought back to our normal dimensions, to the most mortifying, the most devastating certitude.

＊

What an incitation to hilarity, hearing the word *goal* while following a funeral procession!

*

We have always been dying, and yet death has lost none of its freshness, its originality. Herein lies the secret of secrets.

*

To read is to let someone else work for you — the most delicate form of exploitation.

*

Anyone who quotes us from memory — and incorrectly — is a saboteur who should be taken to court. A garbled quotation is equivalent to a betrayal, an insult, a prejudice all the more serious in that the intention was to do us a favor.

*

The tormented — who are they, if not martyrs embittered by not knowing for whose sake to immolate themselves?

*

To think is to submit to the whims and commands of an uncertain health.

*

Having begun my day with Meister Eckhart, I then turned to Epicurus. And the day is not yet over; with whom shall I end it?

*

Once I emerge from the "I," I put myself to sleep.

*

Who does not believe in Fate proves he has not lived.

*

If I should ever happen to die one of these days . . .

*

A middle-aged woman, passing me on the street, took it into her head to announce, without looking at me, "To-day I see nothing but walking corpses wherever I look." Then, still without looking at me, she added, "I'm crazy, aren't I, Monsieur?"

"Not all that crazy," I replied, with a glance of complicity.

*

To see in every baby a future Richard III . . .

*

At every age of our life, we discover that life is a mistake. Only at fifteen is this a revelation that combines a shudder of fear and a touch of enchantment. With time this revelation, degenerating, turns into to a truism, and thus we come to regret the period when it was a source of the unforeseen.

*

In the spring of 1937, as I was walking on the grounds of the psychiatric hospital of Sibiu, in Transylvania, a "pensioner" approached me. We exchanged a few words, and then I said to him, "It's pleasant here."

"I know — it's worth the trouble of being crazy," he replied.

"But still, you are in a sort of prison."

"If you like, but we live here quite without anxiety. Besides, there's a war coming; you know that as well as I do. And this is a safe place. We won't be called up, and they never bomb insane asylums. If I were you, I'd get myself committed right away." Troubled, amazed, I left him and tried to find out something more about my interlocutor. I was assured that he was genuinely mad. Mad or not, no one has ever given me more reasonable advice.

*

It is flawed humanity that constitutes the substance of literature. The writer congratulates himself upon Adam's perversity and prospers only to the degree that each of us assumes and renews it.

*

As for biological patrimony, the merest innovation is, it would seem, a disaster. Life is conservative and flourishes only through repetition, through cliché, through formula. Just the contrary of art.

*

Ghenghis Khan took along the greatest Taoist sage of his time on all of his expeditions. Extreme cruelty is rarely vulgar; it always has something strange and refined about it that inspires fear and respect. William the Conqueror, as pitiless to his allies as he was to his enemies, liked only wild beasts and dark forests where he would always walk alone.

*

I was about to go out when, in order to tie my scarf, I glanced at myself in the mirror. Suddenly an unspeakable terror: *who is that?* Impossible to recognize myself. Though I had no trouble identifying my overcoat, my necktie, my hat, I couldn't make out who I was, for I was not *myself* — *that* was not me. This lasted a certain number of seconds: twenty, thirty, forty? When I managed to come to my senses, the terror persisted. I had to wait for it to consent to disappear.

*

An oyster, to build up its shell, must pass its weight in seawater through its body fifty thousand times. . . . Where have I turned for my lessons in patience!

*

Read somewhere the statement "God speaks only of

Himself." On this specific point, the Almighty has more than one rival.

*

To be or not to be.

. . . Neither one nor the other.

*

Each time I happen upon even the merest sentence of Buddhist lore, I am overcome by a desire to return to that wisdom, which I have tried to absorb for quite a long period of time and which, inexplicably, I have partially forsaken. In that wisdom abides not so much truth as something better still . . . and it is by that wisdom we accede to the state where we are purified of all things, of illusions first of all. No longer to have any such thing, yet not to risk ruin, to sink into disillusion while avoiding bitterness, to be a little more emancipated every day from the obnubilation in which these living hordes languish. . . .

*

To die is to change genre, to renew oneself. . . .

*

Beware of thinkers whose minds function only when they are fueled by a quotation.

*

If relations between men are so difficult, it is because men have been created to knock each other down and not to have "relations."

*

Conversation with him was as conventional as with a dying man.

*

Ceasing to exist signifies nothing, can signify nothing. What is the use of being concerned with what survives a nonreality, with a semblance that succeeds another

semblance? Death is in fact nothing, it is at most a simulacrum of mystery, like life itself. Antimetaphysical pro-
paganda of the graveyards.

*

In my childhood, there was one figure I could never
forget, a peasant who, having just inherited some money,
went from tavern to tavern, followed by a "musician." A
splendid summer day: the whole village was in the fields;
he alone, accompanied by his violinist, wandered the
empty streets, humming some tune. After two years, he
was as poor as before. But the gods were kind: he died
soon after. Without knowing why, I was fascinated, and
rightly so. When I think of him now, I still believe he was
really someone; of all the inhabitants of the village, he
alone had enough imagination to ruin his life.

*

Longing to yell, to spit in people's faces, to drag them
along the ground, to trample them . . . I have trained
myself to decency in order to humble my rage, and my
rage takes revenge as often as it can.

*

If I were asked to summarize as briefly as possible my
vision of things, to reduce it to its most succinct expression, I should replace words with an exclamation point, a
definitive *!*

*

Doubt creeps in everywhere, with, however, a signal
exception: there is no *skeptical* music.

*

Demosthenes copied out Thucydides eight times. That
is how you learn a language. One ought to have the courage to transcribe all the books one loves.

*

That someone should detest what we do, we tolerate, more or less. But if someone disdains a book we have recommended to him, that is much more serious, and it wounds us like an underhanded attack. For then it is our taste that is called into question, and even our discernment!

*

When I *observe* how I slide into sleep, I have the impression of sinking into a providential abyss, of falling into it for eternity, without ever being able to escape. Moreover, no desire to escape even touches me. What I desire in such moments is to perceive them as clearly as possible, to lose nothing of them, and to enjoy them until the last, before unconsciousness, before beatitude.

*

The last important poet of Rome, Juvenal, and the last decisive writer of Greece, Lucian, both *labored* in irony. Two literatures that ended thus — as everything, literature or not, ought to end.

*

This return to the inorganic ought not to affect us in any fashion. Yet so lamentable, not to say so laughable a phenomenon makes cowards of us all. It is time to *rethink* death, to imagine a less mediocre downfall.

*

Astray here on earth, as I would doubtless be astray anywhere.

*

There cannot be *pure* sentiments between those who follow similar paths. One need merely recall the glances we cast at each other when we share the same sidewalk.

*

One grasps incomparably more things in boredom

than by labor, *effort* being the mortal enemy of medi-tation.

*

To shift from scorn to detachment seems easy enough. Yet this is not so much a transition as a feat, an accomplishment. Scorn is the first victory over the world; detachment the last, the supreme. The interval separating them is identified with the path leading from liberty to liberation.

*

I have never met one deranged mind that lacked curiosity about God. Are we to conclude from this that there exists a link between the search for the absolute and the disaggregation of the brain?

*

Any maggot to regard itself as first among its peers would immediately assume the status of man.

*

If everything were to be erased from my mind except the traces of what I have known as unique, where would these come from if not from the thirst for nonexistence?

*

How many missed opportunities to compromise myself with God!

*

Overwhelming joy, if extended, is closer to madness than is the persistent melancholy which justifies itself by reflection and even by mere observation, whereas joy's excesses derive from some derangement. If it is disconcerting to be happy over the mere fact of being alive, it is quite normal, on the other hand, to be sad even before learning baby talk.

*

The luck of the novelist or the playwright: to express himself by disguising himself, to release himself from his conflicts and, still more, from all those characters brawling within himself! Things turn out otherwise for the essayist, faced with a problematic genre into which he projects his own incompatibilities only by contradicting himself at every step. One is freer in the aphorism — triumph of a disintegrated ego. . . .

✳

I am thinking at this moment of someone whom I used to admire unreservedly, who kept none of his promises and who, by disappointing all those who believed in him, died in a virtual paroxysm of satisfaction.

✳

Language compensates for the inadequacy of remedies and cures most of our diseases. The chatterbox does not haunt pharmacies.

✳

Stupefying lack of necessity: life, improvisation, fantasy of matter, ephemeral chemistry. . . .

✳

Love's great (and sole) originality is to make happiness indistinct from misery.

✳

Letters, letters to write. This one, for instance . . . but I cannot do it: I suddenly feel myself incapable of *lying*.

✳

On this estate dedicated, like its manor house, to the crackbrained enterprises of charity, everywhere one looks there are old women kept alive by virtue of surgical operations. There was a time when one died at home, in the dignity of solitude and desertion; now the moribund are collected, crammed, and their indecent throes extended as long as possible.

*

No sooner have we lost one defect than another presses forward to take its place. Such is the price of our equilibrium.

*

Words have become so external to me that making contact with them assumes the proportions of a feat. We have nothing more to say to one another, and if I employ them still, it is to denounce them, while secretly deploring an ever-imminent rupture.

*

At the Luxembourg, a woman of about forty, almost elegant but with a certain bizarre look about her, was speaking in an affectionate, even impassioned tone to someone who was not to be seen. As I caught up with her, I noticed that she was clutching a marmoset to her bosom. She then sat down on a bench, where she continued her monologue with the same intensity. The first words I heard as I passed her were: "You know, I've had about enough." I walked on, not knowing whom to pity more: her or her confidant.

*

That man *is going to* disappear has been, heretofore, my firm conviction. But now I've changed my mind: he *must* disappear.

*

Aversion to all that is human is compatible with pity; I should even say that these reactions are interdependent but not simultaneous. Only someone who knows the former is capable of intensely experiencing the latter.

*

Just now, the sensation of being the last version of the

Universe: worlds revolved around me, yet I felt not the slightest trace of disequilibrium, only something far *above* what it is licit to experience.

*

Waking with a start, wondering if the word *sense* has any meaning, then astounded not to be able to fall asleep again!

*

It is characteristic of pain not to be ashamed of repeating itself.

*

To that very old friend who informs me of his decision to put an end to his days, I reply that he mustn't be in any hurry, that the game's ending is not without a charm of its own, and that one can even come to terms with the Intolerable, provided one never forgets that everything is a bluff, a bluff that generates torments. . . .

*

He worked and produced, he flung himself into massive generalizations, astonished by his own fecundity. He was quite ignorant, fortunately for him, of the nightmare of nuance.

*

To exist is a deviation so patent that it acquires thereby the prestige of a longed-for infirmity.

*

To recognize in oneself all the vile instincts of which one is ashamed. . . . If they are so energetic in someone who strives to be rid of them, how much more virulent must they be in those who, lacking a minimum of lucidity, will never manage to be on their guard, and still less to loathe themselves!

*

In the heat of success or of failure, remember how we

were conceived. Incomparable recipe for triumphing over euphoria or discontent.

*

Only the plant approaches "wisdom"; the animal is unsuited to it. As for man . . . Nature should have stopped with the vegetable kingdom, instead of disqualifying herself by a craving for the extraordinary.

*

The young and the old, and the others too — all odious, they can be brought to heel only by flattery, which ends by making them more odious still.

*

"Heaven is open to no one . . . it will open only after the disappearance of the world" (Tertullian). One is speechless that after such a warning, we have continued our agitation. Of what obstinancy is history the fruit!

*

Dorotea von Rodde-Schloezer, accompanying her husband, the mayor of Lübeck, to Napoleon's coronation, wrote, "There are so many madmen on earth, and especially in France, that it is child's play for this Corsican prestidigitator to make them dance like marionettes to the sound of his pipe. They all fling themselves after this rat charmer, and no one asks where he is leading them." Periods of expansion are periods of delirium; periods of decadence and recession are by comparison reasonable, even too reasonable, and that is why they are almost as deadly as the others.

*

Opinions, yes; convictions, no. That is the point of departure for an intellectual pride.

*

We are all the more attached to someone when his instinct for self-preservation is ambivalent, not to say obliterated.

*

Lucretius: we know nothing specific about his life. Specific? Not even vague. An enviable destiny.

*

Nothing comparable to the onset of depression at the moment of waking. It takes one back billions of years, back to the first signs, to the prodromes of Being — indeed, back to the very *principle* of depression.

*

"You have no need to end up on the Cross, for you were born crucified" (December 11, 1963). What would I not give to recall what could have provoked a despair so overweening!

*

We recall Pascal's frenzy, in *The Provincial Letters*, over the casuist Escobar, who, according to a French traveler visiting him on the Iberian peninsula, knew nothing of these attacks. Further, Pascal was scarcely known in his own country. Misunderstanding and unreality, wherever one looks.

*

So many friends and enemies, who showed an equal interest in us, vanished one after the next. What a relief! To be able to let oneself go at last, no longer having to fear their censure or their disappointment.

*

To pass irreconcilable judgments upon anything, including death, is the sole manner of not cheating.

*

According to Asanga and his school, the triumph of good over evil is merely a victory of *maya* over *maya;*

similarly, putting an end to transmigration by illumination is like "a king of illusion vanquishing a king of illusion" (*Mahayanasutralamkara*).

These Hindus have had the audacity to set illusion so high, to make it a substitute for self and world, and to convert it into the supreme given. Remarkable conversion, ultimate and inescapable stage. What is to be done? Every extremity, even liberation, being an impasse, how to escape in order to catch up with the Possible? Perhaps one must lower the terms of the debate, endow things with a shadow of reality, restrain the hegemony of clear-sightedness, dare to maintain that everything that seems to exist *does exist* in its way, and then, weary of wandering off the point, change the subject. . . .

10

Mircea Eliade

*

I FIRST MET ELIADE around 1932, in Bucharest, where I had just finished some sort of studies in philosophy. He was at that time the idol of the "new generation," a magic formula we were proud to invoke. We scorned the "old," the "dodderers" — anyone over thirty. Our intellectual leader waged a campaign against them; he demolished them one by one, striking almost always to the heart (I say "almost" because occasionally he missed his aim, as when he attacked Tudor Arghezi, a great poet whose only fault was to be acclaimed, consecrated). The struggle between generations seemed to us the key to every conflict and the explanatory principle of every event. To be young, for us, was automatically to have genius. Such infatuation, it will be said, is universal. No doubt. But I don't think it was ever carried so far as it was with us: in it was expressed, was exacerbated, a determination to force History, an appetite to find our place within it and to effect the New at any price. Frenzy was the order of the day. In whom was it embodied? In someone who had returned from India, from the country that has always and specifically turned its back on History, on chronology, on Becoming as such. I should not point out this paradox if it did not testify to a profound duality, to a character trait in Eliade, equally solicited by essence and by accident, the timeless and the quotidian, mysticism and literature. This duality involves no laceration for him: it is his nature and his luck to be able to live simultaneously or alternately on different spiritual levels, to ponder ecstasy and pursue anecdotes without making a fuss.

In the period when I knew him, I was already amazed that he could be studying Sankhya (about which he had just published a long article) and also be interested in the latest novel. Subsequently I have never failed to be amazed by the spectacle of a curiosity so immense and so intense; in anyone else it would be morbid. He has nothing of the grim and perverse obstinacy of the maniac, of the obsessive who limits himself to a single realm, to a single sector, and rejects all the rest as secondary and trivial. The one obsession I recognize in him — and in truth it has diminished with the years — is that of the polygraph, the universal writer, hence of the anti-obsessive par excellence, since he is eager to fling himself upon any subject in his unquenchable thirst for exploration. Nicolas Iorga, the Rumanian historian — an extraordinary figure, fascinating and dismaying, the author of over a thousand works that in places are extremely lively but in general are confused, poorly constructed, unreadable, shot through with flashes of wit smothered in tedium — in those days Eliade admired him passionately, the way one admires the elements, a forest, the sea, the fields, fecundity itself, everything that burgeons, proliferates, erupts, and asserts itself. The superstition of vitality and productivity, especially in literature, has never left him. I may be speaking out of

turn here, but I have every reason to believe that in his
unconscious, he sets books above the gods: more than to
the latter, it is to books that he addresses his worship. In
any case, I have met no one who loved them so much as
he. I shall never forget the fever with which, arriving in
Paris just after the liberation, he touched them, caressed
them, leafed through them; in bookstores he exulted, he
officiated; it was something like enchantment, idolatry. So
much enthusiasm presupposes a great depth of generosity,
a defect of which one cannot determine the profusion, the
exuberance, the prodigality — all qualities thanks to
which the mind *imitates* and exceeds nature. I have never
been able to read Balzac; to tell the truth, I stopped trying
on the threshold of adolescence. His world is closed to me,
inaccessible; I never manage to enter it; I am refractory to
it. How many times has Eliade tried to convert me! He
first read the *Comédie humaine* in Bucharest; he reread it
in Paris in 1947; perhaps he is rereading it in Chicago
now. He has always loved ample, exuberant novels that
unfold on several levels, accompanying the "endless" mel-
ody, the massive presence of time, the accumulation of
details and the abundance of complex and divergent
themes; on the other hand, he has no use for anything, in
letters, that is *exercise,* the anemic and refined games aes-
thetes play, the overripe, *faisandé* aspect of certain productions lacking in instinct and in juice. But one can also
explain his passion for Balzac in another way. There are
two kinds of minds: those that love process and those that
love the result. The first are attached to the unfolding, the
stages, the successive expressions of thought or of action;
the second, to the final expression, except for which
nothing matters. By temperament I have always been inclined toward the latter, toward a Chamfort, a Joubert, a

Lichtenberg, who give you a formula without revealing the path that has led them to it. Whether out of modesty or out of sterility, they cannot free themselves from the superstition of concision; they want to say everything in a page, a phrase, a word; sometimes they succeed, though rarely, it must be said: laconism must resign itself to silence if it wants to avoid a fake enigmatic profundity. Still, when one lives this quintessentialized — or sclerotic — form of expression, it is difficult to wrest oneself away from it and to care much for any other variety. He who has frequented the moralists for a long time will have difficulty understanding Balzac, but he can divine the reasons of those who have a great weakness for him, who derive from his universe a sensation of life, of expansion, of freedom, unknown to the lover of maxims, a minor genre in which perfection is identified with asphyxia.

However distinct Eliade's taste for huge syntheses, it is just as clear that he might also have excelled in the fragment, in the brief and brilliant essay; indeed, he has done so: witness his first productions, that multitude of succinct texts he published both before his departure for India and after his return. In 1927 and 1928, he contributed regularly to a Bucharest daily. I was living in a provincial town, where I was completing my secondary studies; the paper was delivered there at eleven in the morning. During recess I would rush to the kiosk to buy it, and that was how I became familiar with the more or less exotic names of Asvaghosha, Ksoma of Koros, Buonaiutti, Eugenio d'Ors, and so many more. I much preferred the articles about foreigners because their works, not to be found in my little town, seemed so mysterious and definitive; happiness for me was the hope of reading them someday.

Eventual disappointment was therefore remote, whereas it was within arm's reach with the native writers. How much erudition, how much vigor and verve were poured out in those fugitive articles! I am sure that they were throbbing with life, with interest, and that I am not exaggerating their value by the distortions of memory. I read them as an enthusiast, it is true, but as a lucid enthusiast. What I particularly valued was the young Eliade's gift for making every idea vivid, contagious, for investing each with a halo of hysteria — but a hysteria that was positive, stimulating, healthy. It is clear that this gift is entirely that of a certain time of life, and that even if one still possesses it beyond that time, one prefers to display it only when one takes up the history of religions. . . . Nowhere was it more evident than in those "Letters to a Provincial Reader" that Eliade wrote after his return from India and that appeared in installments in the same daily. I don't think I missed a single one of those letters; I read them all — indeed, we all read them, for they concerned us, they were addressed to us. Most often we were taken to task, and each of us waited our turn. One day mine came. I was invited to do nothing less than liquidate my obsessions, cease invading the periodicals with my grim notions, deal with other problems than that of death, my fixation then as always. Would I yield to such a challenge? I had no intention of doing so. I was reluctant to admit that one could address any problem other than this one: I had just published a text on the "vision of death in northern art," and I planned to persevere in the same direction. In my heart of hearts I blamed my friend for not identifying himself with something, indeed for identifying himself with nothing, for trying to be *everything* since he was unable to be some-thing — for being, in short, incapable of fanaticism, of delirium, of "depth," by which I meant the faculty of giving oneself up to an obsession and standing by it. I imagined that to be *something* was to assume an attitude totally, and therefore to reject availability, entertainment, any perpetual renewal. To create a world for oneself, a limited absolute, and to cling to it with all one's might — that seemed to me the ultimate intellectual duty. It was the notion of commitment, of *engagement,* if you will, but engagement that had the inner life as its sole object, a commitment to myself and not to others. I reproached Eliade for being elusive because he was so open, so mobile, so enthusiastic. I also reproached him for not being interested exclusively in India; it seemed to me that India could effectively replace all the rest, and that it was a falling-off to be concerned with anything else. All these grievances were embodied in an article with the agressive title "The Man without a Destiny," in which I assailed the instability of this figure I so admired, his inability to be a man of one idea; I set forth the negative aspect of each of his virtues (which is the classical way of being unjust and disloyal to someone), I blamed him for mastering his moods and his passions, for being able to use them as he liked, for spiriting away the tragic, and for being unaware of "fatality." This formal attack had the defect of being too general: it might have been launched against anyone. Why should a theoretical mind, a man absorbed by problems, figure as a hero or a monster? There is no affinity of substance between ideas and tragedy. But at the time I thought that every idea must incarnate itself or turn into a lyric cry. Convinced that discouragement was the very sign of awakening, of awareness, I castigated my friend for being too optimistic, for being interested in too many things, and for manifesting an activity incompatible with the demands of true knowledge. Because I was abulic, I believed myself more advanced than he, as if my abulia were the result of a spiritual conquest or a will-to-wisdom. I remember telling him once that in a previous life he must have fed entirely on greens, to be able to preserve so much freshness and trust, and so much innocence too. I could not forgive him for the fact that I felt older than he; I held him responsible for my acrimony and my fiascos, and it seemed to me that he had acquired his hopes at the expense of mine. How could he function in so many different sectors? It was his curiosity — in which I saw a demon or, with Saint Augustine, a "disease" — that was my invariable grievance. But in him curiosity was not a disease; on the contrary, it was a sign of health. And I blamed him for that health and envied it at the same time. But here I must be permitted a little indiscretion.

I should probably not have dared to write "The Man without a Destiny" if a special circumstance had not determined me to do so. We had a mutual friend, an actress of great talent who, unfortunately for her, was obsessed with metaphysical problems. This obsession eventually compromised both her talent and her career. On the stage, right in the middle of a scene, her essential preoccupations would overwhelm her, invade her, seize her mind, so that what she was saying suddenly seemed of an intolerable inanity. Her performances suffered; she was much too obsessed to be able to change, or to want to change. She was not dismissed, merely given minor parts that would cause her no difficulties at all. She took advantage of this to devote herself to her interrogations and her speculative tastes, bringing to them all the passion she had deployed in the theater. Seeking answers, she turned in her confusion to Eliade, then — less inspired — to me. One day, unable to stand it anymore, he sent her away and refused to see her again. She came to tell me her disappointments, and after that I saw her often, listening as she talked. She was dazzling, it is true, but so all-absorbing, so wearing, so insistent, that after each of our meetings I would go to the nearest bistro and get drunk, exasperated and fascinated. A peasant girl (for she was an autodidact who had grown up in a godforsaken village) who talked to you about Nothingness with such brio, such fervor! She had learned several languages, dabbled in theosophy, read the great poets, experienced a good number of disappointments, though none had affected her so much as the last. Her merits, like her torments, were such that at the beginning of my friendship with her, it seemed to me inexplicable and inadmissible that Eliade should have treated her so cavalierly. Regarding his behavior toward her as inexcusable, I wrote, to avenge her, "The Man without a Destiny." When the article appeared on the first page of a monthly, she was delighted by it, read it aloud in my presence as if it were some glamorous *tirade,* and then proceeded to analyze it paragraph by paragraph. "You've never written anything better," she told me — misplaced praise she was actually bestowing on herself, for was it not she who had somehow provoked the article and provided me with its elements? Subsequently I understood Eliade's weariness and exasperation with her, and the absurdity of my excessive attack, which he never held against me, which even amused him. This character trait deserves note, for experience has taught me that writers — all afflicted with prodigious memory — are incapable of forgetting an overly wounding impertinence.

It was during this same period that he began teaching at the Faculty of Letters in Bucharest. I attended his lectures whenever I could. The fervor he lavished on his articles was fortunately recognizable in his lectures, the most animated, the most vibrant I have ever heard. Without notes, without anything, swept on by a vertigo of lyric erudition, he was a fountain of convulsed yet coherent words, underlined by the spasmodic movements of his hands. An hour of tension, after which, miraculously, he did not seem tired and perhaps, indeed, was not. It was as if he possessed the art of indefinitely postponing fatigue. Everything *negative*, everything that incites to self-destruction on the physical as well as the spiritual plane, was then, and is now, alien to him — whence his inaptitude for resignation, for remorse, for all the sentiments that imply impasse, stagnation, non-future. Once again I may be speaking out of turn, but I believe that if he has a perfect comprehension of sin, he has no sense of it: he is too febrile for that, too dynamic, too hurried, too full of projects, too intoxicated by the possible. Only those have such a sense who endlessly ruminate upon their past, who fasten themselves to it and are unable to tear themselves away, who invent defects out of a need for moral torment and delight in the memory of any shameful or irreparable action they have committed or, above all, wanted to commit. Obsessives, to speak of them further. They alone have time to descend into the abysses of remorse, to sojourn there, to wallow there; they alone are kneaded of that substance out of which the authentic Christian is made — that is, someone ravaged, corroded from within, suffering the morbid desire to be a reprobate and ending all the same by overcoming that desire, such a victory, never complete, being what he calls "having faith." Since Pascal and Kierkegaard, we can no longer conceive of "salvation" without a procession of infirmities, and without the secret pleasures of the interior drama. Today especially, since "malediction" is in vogue — it is literature we are discussing — we would have everyone live in anguish and anathema. But can a man of learning be *accursed?* And why should he be? Does he not know too much to condescend to hell and its narrow circles? It is virtually certain that only the dark aspects of Christianity still rouse a certain echo in us. Perhaps Christianity, if we would regain its essence, must be seen, in fact, *en noir*. If this image, this vision, is correct, Eliade is from all appearances marginal to this religion. But perhaps he is marginal to *all* religions, as much by profession as by conviction: is he not one of the most brilliant representatives of a new Alexandrianism that, after the fashion of the old, puts all beliefs on the same level, without being able to adopt any? Once we refuse to hierarchize them, which are we to prefer, which adopt, and which divinity invoke? One does not imagine a specialist in the history of religions *at prayer*. Or if indeed he does pray, then he belies his teaching, contradicts himself, ruins his *Treatises,* in which no *true* god figures, in which all gods are on equal footing. Though he describes and discusses them with all the talent in the world, he cannot inspire them with life; he will have extracted all their sap, he will have compared them to each other, scoured them against each other, to their great detriment, and what will be left of them is anemic symbols with which a believer can do nothing — if at this stage of erudition, of disillusion and of irony, there can still be someone who truly believes. We are all, Eliade first of all, *ci-devant* believers; we are all religious spirits without religion.

11

That Fatal Perspicacity

＊

ᴇACH EVENT is only one more bad sign. Occasionally, though, an exception does occur — which the chronicler exaggerates to create the illusion of the unexpected.

＊

That envy is universal is best proved by the fact that it breaks out among the mad themselves in their brief intervals of lucidity.

＊

Every anomaly seduces us, Life in the first place, that anomaly par excellence.

＊

Standing, one readily admits that every passing moment vanishes forever; *prone,* this obvious point seems so inadmissible that we long never to get up again.

＊

Progress and the Eternal Return: two meaningless things. What remains? Resignation to becoming, to surprises that are no such thing, to calamities that pretend to be uncommon.

＊

If we began by doing away with all those who can breathe only on a platform!

*

Vehement by nature, vacillating by choice. Which way to tend? With *whom* to side? What *self* to join?

*

Our virtues and our vices must be tenacious to keep themselves on the surface, to safeguard that enterprising style we need in order to resist the glamour of destruction or despair.

*

"You speak of God frequently. It is a word I no longer use," an ex-nun writes me. Not everyone has the good fortune to be disgusted by it!

*

In the still of certain nights, for lack of a confidant, we are reduced to the One who played this part for centuries, for millennia.

*

Irony, that nuanced, rancorous impertinence, is the art of being able to stop. The merest probe beneath the surface destroys it. If you have a tendency to insist, you run the risk of capsizing with it.

*

What is marvelous is that each day brings us a new reason to disappear.

*

Since the only things we remember are humiliations and defeats, what is the use of all the rest?

*

To inquire into the basis of anything makes one long to throw oneself on the ground. In any case, that is how I used to answer the crucial questions, questions without an answer.

*

Opening this textbook on prehistory, I come across some specimens of our ancestors, as grim as could be. Doubtless they had to be so. Disgusted and ashamed, I quickly close the book, realizing I will open it again whenever I want to dwell on the genesis of our horrors and our filth.

*

The secret life of anti-life, and this chemical comedy, instead of inclining us to smile, gnaws at our vitals and maddens us.

*

The need to devour oneself absolves one of the need to believe.

*

If fury were an attribute of the Almighty, I should long since have transcended my mortal status.

*

Existence might be justified if each of us behaved as if he were the last man alive.

*

Ignatius of Loyola, tormented by scruples whose nature he does not specify, tells us that he considered destroying himself. Even he! This temptation is certainly more widespread and more deeply rooted than is realized. It is in fact the honor of mankind, until it becomes the duty.

*

To create: only someone mistaken about himself, someone ignorant of the secret motives behind his actions, *creates*. Once the creator is transparent to himself, he no longer creates. Self-knowledge antagonizes the *demon*. Here is where we must seek out the reason that Socrates wrote nothing.

*

That we can be wounded by the very people we despise discredits pride.

*

In a work admirably translated from English, just one blemish: "*les abîmes du scepticism,*" for which the translator should have supplied *doute,* for in French the word *skepticism* has a nuance of dilettantism, even frivolity, not to be associated with the notion of the abyss.

*

A taste for formula goes along with a weakness for definitions, for whatever has least relation to reality.

*

Everything that can be classified is perishable. Only what is susceptible to several interpretations endures.

*

To confront the blank page — what a Waterloo prospect!

*

In conversation with someone, whatever his merits may be, never forget for a moment that in his profound reactions he is no different from ordinary mortals. For discretion's sake, you must handle him carefully, for like anyone else, he will not tolerate frankness, direct cause of almost all quarrels and grudges.

*

To have grazed every form of failure, including success.

*

We haven't a single letter of Shakespeare's. Didn't he write any? One would have liked to hear Hamlet complain about his mail.

*

The eminent virtue of calumny is that it produces a vacuum around you without your having to raise a finger.

*

Desperate disgust in the presence of a crowd, whether high-spirited or sullen.

*

Everything is in decline, and always has been. Once this diagnosis is well established, you can utter any enormity; you are even obliged to.

*

If you are almost always overcome by events, it is because you need merely wait in order to realize that you have been guilty of naïveté.

*

The passion for music is in itself an admission. We know more about a stranger who abandons himself to it than about someone indifferent to it whom we deal with every day.

*

Dead of night. No one, nothing but the society of the moments. Each pretends to keep us company, then escapes — desertion after desertion.

*

To side with things testifies to an upsetting perturbation. To say "living" is to say "partial": objectivity, a belated phenomenon, an alarming symptom, is the first stage of capitulation.

*

One would have to be as unenlightened as an angel or an idiot to imagine that the human escapade could turn out well.

*

A neophyte's virtues are accentuated and reinforced under the effect of his new convictions. He knows this; what he does not know is that his faults increase proportionately. The source of his chimeras and his vainglory.

*

"My children, salt comes from water, and if it comes in contact with water, it dissolves and vanishes. In the same way, the monk is born of woman, and if he approaches a woman, he dissolves and ceases to be a monk." This Jean Moschus, in the seventh century, seems to have understood better than either Strindberg or Weininger the danger already pointed out in Genesis.

*

Every *life* is the story of a collapse. If biographies are so fascinating, it is because the heroes, and the cowards quite as much, strive to innovate in the art of debacle.

*

Disappointed by everyone, it is inevitable that we should eventually be so by ourselves — unless that is how we began.

*

"Since I first began to observe men, I have learned only to love them more," writes Lavater, a contemporary of Chamfort. Such a remark, normal for an inhabitant of a Swiss village, might have seemed of an indecorous simplicity to a frequenter of Parisian salons.

*

Regret at not having been deceived like all the rest, rage at having seen clearly: such is the secret misery of more than one enlightened person.

*

How could I resign myself even for a moment to what is not eternal? Yet this happens to me — at this very moment, for example.

*

Each of us clings as best he can to his unlucky star.

*

The older one grows, the more clearly one realizes that

though one believes oneself liberated from everything, in reality one is liberated from nothing.

*

On a gangrened planet, we should abstain from making plans, but we make them still, optimism being, as we know, a dying man's reflex.

*

Meditation is a waking state sustained by a dim disturbance, which is at once ravage and benediction.

*

He could not put up with living in God's wake.

*

Original Sin and Transmigration: both identify destiny with an *expiation,* and it is of no matter whether we are talking about Adam's sin or those we committed in our previous existences.

*

The last leaves dance as they fall. It takes a big dose of insensitivity to confront autumn.

*

We imagine we are advancing toward some goal, forgetting that we really advance only toward The Goal itself, toward the discomfiture of all the others.

*

Never unreal, Pain is a challenge to the universal fiction. What luck to be the only sensation granted a content, if not a meaning!

*

Despondency. This English word, charged with all the nuances of collapse, will have been the key to my years, the emblem of my moments, of my negative courage, of my invalidation of all tomorrows.

*

When we have no further desire to show ourselves, we take refuge in music, that Providence of the abulic.

*

The reasons for persisting in Being seem less and less well founded, and our successors will find it easier than we to be rid of such obstinacy.

*

Once we are grazed by certainty, we no longer mistrust ourselves and others. Confidence, in all its forms, is a source of action, hence of error.

*

When we encounter someone *actual,* our surprise is such that we wonder if we are not the victim of some vertigo.

*

What is the use of combing works of consolation, since they are legion and since only two or three count?

*

If you don't want to explode with rage, leave your memory alone, abstain from burrowing there.

*

Whatever follows the laws of life — hence whatever decays — inspires me with reflections so contradictory that they border on mental confusion.

*

To live in fear of being bored to death everywhere, even in God: this obsession with boredom imposes limits; in it I see the reason for my spiritual unfulfillment.

*

Between Epicurism and Stoicism, which are we to choose? I shift from one to the other and most often am faithful to both at once — which is my way of espousing the maxims Antiquity preferred to the swarming of dogmas.

*

*

It is to our inertia that we owe our rescue from the inflation into which more than one man falls out of an excess of vanity, labor, or talent. If it is not comforting, it is in any case flattering to tell ourselves that we shall die without having given our measure.

*

To have shouted one's doubts from the rooftops, even while siding with that school of discretion which is skepticism.

*

The considerable service done us by pests, thieves of our time, who keep us from leaving behind a complete image of our capacities.

*

It is praiseworthy for us to love anything and anyone except our kind, precisely because they resemble ourselves. This phenomenon suffices to explain why history is what it is.

*

Most of our evils issue from a great distance, from this or that ancestor ruined by his excesses. We are punished for his dissipations: no need to drink, he will have drunk in our place. That hangover which so surprises us is the price we pay for his euphorias.

*

Thirty years of ecstasy at the altar of the Cigarette. Now, when I see others sacrifice to my former idol, I do not understand them, I regard them as unhinged or defective. If a "vice" we have conquered becomes alien to us to such a degree, how can we fail to be astounded by those we have not practiced?

*

In order to deceive melancholy, you must keep moving. Once you stop, it wakens, if in fact it has ever dozed off.

*

The desire to work comes over me only when I have an appointment. I always go off feeling certain I am missing a unique opportunity to outdo myself.

*

"I cannot do without the things I care nothing for," the Duchess du Maine liked to say. Frivolity, to this degree, is a prelude to renunciation.

*

If the Almighty could realize how burdensome the merest action is to me on some occasions, He would not fail, in an impulse of pity, to yield me His place.

*

Not knowing which way to turn, preferring a discontinuous reflection, image of time broken into pieces. . . .

*

What I *know* wreaks havoc upon what I *want*.

*

Returning home after a cremation: instant devaluation of Eternity and all the other great words.

*

Nameless prostration, then dilation beyond the limits of the world and the resistance of the mind.

*

The thought of death enslaves those whom it haunts. It liberates only at the beginning; then it degenerates into an obsession, thereby ceasing to be a thought.

*

The world is an accident of God, *accidens Dei*. How right the formula of Albertus Magnus seems!

*

By virtue of depression, we recall those misdeeds we buried in the depths of our memory. Depression exhumes our shames.

*

In our veins flows the blood of monkeys. If we were to think of it often, we should end by giving up. No more theology, no more metaphysics — which comes down to saying no more divagations, no more arrogance, no more excess, no more anything. . . .

*

Is it conceivable to adhere to a religion founded by *someone else?*

*

Tolstoy's excuse as a preacher is that he had two disciples who derived the practical consequences of his homilies: Wittgenstein and Gandhi. The first gave away his possessions; the second had none to give away.

*

The world begins and ends with us. Only our consciousness exists, it is everything, and this everything vanishes with it. Dying, we leave nothing. Then why so much fuss around an event that is no such thing?

*

There comes a moment when one imitates nothing more than oneself.

*

When you waken with a start and long to get back to sleep, you must dismiss every impulse of thought, any shadow of an idea. For it is the formulated idea, the distinct idea, that is sleep's worst enemy.

*

A hair-raising figure, the misunderstood man brings everything back to himself. His sneers fail to counterbalance the praises that he never ceases to grant himself and

that exceed those not offered him. O for the lucky ones —
rare, it is true — who, having triumphed, are able on occasion to stand aside! In any case, they do not exhaust
themselves in recriminations, and their vanity consoles us
for the arrogance of the misunderstood.

*

If from time to time we are tempted by faith, it is because faith proposes an alternative humiliation: it is, after
all, preferable to find oneself in a position of inferiority
before a god than before a hominid.

*

We can console someone only by following the direction of his affliction, to the point where the afflicted man
can endure being so no longer.

*

So many memories that loom up without apparent necessity — of what use are they, except to show us that
with age we are becoming external to our own life, that
these remote "events" no longer have anything to do with
us, and that one day the same will be true of this life itself?

*

The mystic's "all is nothing" is merely a preliminary to
the absorption in that *all* which becomes miraculously existent — that is, really *all*. This conversion was not to
function in me, the positive, luminous portion of mysticism having been denied me.

*

Between the demand to be clear and the temptation to
be obscure, impossible to decide which deserves more respect.

*

Having scrutinized those we must envy, to realize we
would willingly exchange fates with no one: everyone

reacts in this way. Then how explain that envy is the oldest and least threadbare of infirmities?

*

Not easy to avoid resentment of a friend who has insulted you during a fit of madness. Though you keep telling yourself that *he was not himself,* you react as if, for once, he had revealed a well-kept secret.

*

If Time were a patrimony, a *possession,* death would be the worst form of theft.

*

Not taking revenge only half flatters us, considering that we never know whether our behavior is based on nobility or on cowardice.

*

Knowledge, or the crime of indiscretion.

*

No use counting on the windfall of being alone — always escorted by oneself!

*

Without will, no conflict: no tragedy among the abulic. Yet the failure of will can be experienced more painfully than a tragic destiny.

*

We come to terms one way or another with any fiasco, with the exception of death, fiasco itself.

*

When we have committed some vile action, we hesitate to take it on ourselves, to designate the party responsible; we waste ourselves in endless ruminations, which are only a further vileness, though attenuated by the acrobatics of shame and remorse.

*

The relief of discovering on the threshold of dawn that it is futile to get to the heart of anything at all.

*

If He who is called God were not the symbol par excellence of solitude, I should never have paid Him the slightest attention. But ever intrigued by monsters, how could I neglect their adversary, more alone than any of them?

*

Every victory is more or less a lie; it touches us only on the surface, whereas a defeat, however trivial, affects us in the deepest part of ourselves, where it will make sure it is not forgotten. Thus, whatever happens, we can count on its company.

*

The amount of emptiness I have accumulated, while keeping my individual status — the miracle of not having exploded under the weight of so much nonexistence!

*

Without the perfume of the Incurable that it trails after it, boredom would be the most insupportable of all scourges.

*

Consciousness of my indignity was crushing me. No argument came to oppose, to weaken it. Though I invoked this or that exploit, nothing availed. "You are merely a supernumerary," a self-assured voice kept repeating. Finally, beside myself, I answered with the right panache: "No need to treat me this way; is it really my responsibility to be the sworn enemy of the planet — indeed, of the macrocosm?"

*

To die is to prove one knows one's own interest.

*

The moment that separates itself from all others, that liberates itself from them and betrays them — with what joy do we hail its infidelity!

*

If we knew the *hour* of our brain!

*

Unless everything is changed — which never happens — no one can resolve his contradictions. Death alone helps here, and it is here that it scores points and out-classes life.

*

To have invented the murderous smile. . . .

*

For thousands of years, we were merely mortal. At last we are promoted to the rank of the moribund.

*

To think we could have spared ourselves from living all that we have lived!

*

On this immaculate page, a gnat was making a dash for it. "Why be in such a hurry? Where are you going, what are you looking for? Relax!" I screamed out in the middle of the night. I would have been so pleased to see it collapse! It's harder than you think to gain disciples.

*

To have nothing in common with the Universe, and to wonder by virtue of what disorder one belongs to it.

*

"Why fragments?" one young philosopher reproached me.

"Out of laziness, out of frivolity, out of disgust — but also for other reasons. . . ." And since I was finding none of these, I launched into prolix explanations that sounded serious to him and that ended by convincing him.

*

French: the ideal idiom for translating equivocal sentiments with some delicacy.

*

In a borrowed language, you are *conscious* of words; they exist not in you but outside of you. This interval between yourself and your means of expression explains why it is difficult, even impossible, to be a poet in another language besides your own. How extract a substance from words that are not rooted in you? The newcomer lives on the surface of language; he cannot, in a tongue belatedly learned, translate that subterranean agony from which poetry issues.

*

Devoured by a nostalgia for paradise, without having known a single attack of true faith. . . .

*

Bach in his grave. So I shall have seen him (like so many others) by one of those indiscretions so familiar to grave-diggers and journalists; since then I keep thinking of those skulls that have nothing original about them except that they proclaim the nothingness he denied.

*

So long as there is a single god *standing,* man's task is not done.

*

The kingdom of the Insoluble extends as far as the eye can see. Our satisfaction therein is mitigated, however. What better proof that we are contaminated by hope from the start?

*

After all, I have not wasted my time, I too have fidgeted, like anyone else, in this aberrant universe.

12

Caillois
Fascination of the Mineral

*

CAILLOIS'S EARLY STUDIES were entirely *comme il faut,* to the point of acknowledging his reactions as a disciple — witness the pains he takes in the 1939 foreword to *Man and the Sacred* to reassure his masters, asking them to ignore the last pages of the book, where, exceeding the limits of "positive knowledge," he permits himself several metaphysical developments. Since at this time he appeared to believe in the history of religions, in sociology and ethnology, he might normally have confined himself to one of these fields and ended his career as a scientist and a scholar. That he took another path was due largely to external circumstances, but as always, they do not account for what is essential. It is important to know why, at the outset, he already inclined toward the fragment rather than toward the system, and why, too, he exhibited that horror of massive constructions, that concern for elegance, that felicity of expression, that touch of breathlessness in demonstration, that proportion, finally, of reasoning and rhythm, of theory and seduction. These superior infirmities, these flaws, he might have camouflaged, provided he sacrificed himself, abdicated his singularity (like more than one possessor of "positive knowledge"). Not being disposed to do so, he was to deviate from his first preoccupations, betray or disappoint his masters, follow a personal path, choose diversity, turn away, in short, from science, accessible only to those who know and endure the intoxication of monotony. He would traverse a number of subjects and disciplines — poetry, Marxism, psychoanalysis, dreams, games — never as a dilettante but as an impatient and greedy spirit condemned by irony to *inadhesion* and, frequently, to injustice. One can readily imagine him raging against a theme he has seized upon, a problem he has elucidated, which he will abandon to the scrupulous or the obsessive, as spending any more time on it would strike him as indecent. This exasperation, based on lassitude, exigence, or tact, is the key to his permanent renewal, to his intellectual peregrinations. One cannot help thinking here of a converse procedure, such as that of a Maurice Blanchot, who in the analysis of literary phenomena has brought to the point of heroism or asphyxia the superstition of depth in a rumination that combines the advantages of the vague and the abyss.

I have often wondered whether, in the case of Caillois, the refusal of reassessment (what he calls his "fundamental dispersion") would not make difficult and even impossible any attempt to identify his "true self." He is the contrary of an obsessive, yet only obsessives yield their "true self," for they alone perhaps are sufficiently *limited* to have such a thing. Without attributing to him obsessions that he would reject, I have nonetheless been led to seek *where* he is supremely himself, and which of his books, had he written only that one, would reveal him best and testify that he has pursued and overtaken his own essence. It has seemed to me that Caillois, subject to so many enthusiasms, has encountered only one passion, and that in the work where he describes it, he has divulged the best part of his secret.

When one undertakes a quest in any realm, the sign of finding is a change of tone, those outbursts of lyricism that are not a priori indispensable. *Stones* begins with a preface-hymn and continues, for page after page, on a note of enthusiasm tempered by meticulousness. I leave aside the secondary reasons for this fervor in order to indicate only the principal one, which seems to me to reside in the search and the nostalgia for the primordial, in the obsession with beginnings, with the worlds before man, with a mystery "slower, vaster, and graver than the fate of that transitory species." To hark back not only beyond the human but beyond life itself, to attain to the principle of the ages, to make oneself a contemporary of the immemorial: such is the enterprise of this exalted mineralogist who rejoices when he detects, in a nodule of agate that is abnormally light, the sound of a liquid, water hidden there since the dawn of the planet, "anterior" water, "water of origins," "incorruptible fluid" that gives the sensation to the living man contemplating it that he is but a "dumbfounded intruder" in the universe.

The quest for beginnings is the most important of all those we can undertake. Each of us makes it, if only in brief moments, as if performing this return presented the unique means of recovering and transcending ourselves, of triumphing over ourselves and over everything. It is also the only mode of escape that is not a desertion or a deception. But we have got in the habit of attaching ourselves to the future, of putting apocalypse above cosmogony, of idolizing the explosion and the end, of banking to an absurd degree on the Revolution or the Last Judgment. Would it not be wiser to turn back, toward a chaos much richer than the one we anticipate? It is toward the moment when this initial chaos, gradually subsiding, experimented with form that Caillois chooses to turn, toward that phase where stones, after the "glowing moment of their genesis," became "algebra, vertigo, order." But whether he invokes them burning, melting, or incurably cold, he exhibits, in his description of them, an ardor that is not habitual in him. I am thinking particularly of his almost visionary way of presenting a specimen of native copper taken from Lake Michigan, whose brittle meshes, "at once fragile and hard, offer the imagination the paradox of a hyperbolic sclerosis. They inexplicably transcend the Inert; they add the rigor of death to what never was alive. They inscribe upon the metal's surface the folds of a superfluous, ostentatious, pleonastic shroud."

Reading *Stones,* I found myself wondering more than once if this was not a language sealed inside its own significations, with no reality other than its particular glamour. Under these conditions, why not go see for myself? After all, I have never *looked at* a stone, and as for the ones called "precious," that epithet alone suffices to make me detest them. So I paid a visit to the Hall of Mineralogy and, to my great surprise, discovered that the book had merely told the truth, that it was the work not of a virtuoso but of a guide, determined to grasp *from within* certain solidified marvels, in order to reconstitute, by a scarcely conceivable regression, their state of original indeterminacy. I had just initiated myself into the mineral, during a crucial hour that brought home to me the inanity of being a sculptor or a painter. Having haunted, a few years earlier, the paleontology section of the museum, I felt then that the skeletons on display were so clean as to disgust one with the scandalous precariousness of flesh, that they could by contrast suggest a certain serenity. Yet compared to stones, skeletons are pitiful. But do stones themselves actually afford, as Caillois observes, "several serenities," and will they wield their spellbinding power over him to the end? Will they resist his need for change, his craving for the new, the disease of "dispersion"? In thinking back to the moment of their genesis, he approached an illumination, an unexpected kind of mystical state, an abyss in which to dissolve. This illumination was to be short-lived: once the abyss has been escaped, we are informed very clearly that it contains nothing divine that is not matter, lava, fusion, cosmic tumult. I cannot insist sufficiently on the originality of this failure. We are all, of course, failures in some mystic aspiration; we have all recorded our limits and our impossibilities at the heart of some extreme experience. But if we have tried to explode our temporal shackles, it is because we have frequented the Desert Fathers, Meister Eckhart, or the later Buddhists — whereas it was by brooding over dendrites and pyrites, or by following in reverse the career of a certain quartz, of a certain agate, that Caillois felt himself slide out of time and made contact, beyond the great "technical ordeals," with the "motionless matter of the longest quietude," where he could not continue because his mind, tempted and disappointed by trance, found it impossible to accede to deliverance by Nothing, not even the mineral. He would say it himself in his book, and better still in the conclusion of the *Récit du Délogé,* a revealing text recently published in *Commerce:* "I have attained the ultimate reality, which is not nothingness but the blur that I have become." Hence not nothingness, and we realize why: nothingness is ultimately merely a *purer* version of God, which is why the mystics have plunged into it with such frenzy, as have, moreover, the unbelievers with a certain religious capital. Caillois does not envy the former and would probably shrink from being classed with the latter. He acknowledges himself unsuited for the "illuminating annihilation"; he admits his defeat, his lassitudes, and his resignations; he proclaims and savors his collapse. After the enfeeblement of a fascination, after the orgy and ecstasy of origins — the *superbia* of disarray, the journey into . . . blur.

13

Michaux
The Passion of the Exhaustive

✳

FIFTEEN YEARS AGO, Michaux would take me regularly to the Grand Palais, where all sorts of scientific films were shown — some curious, others technical, impenetrable. To tell the truth, I was intrigued less by the projections than by the interest my friend took in them. I could not understand the motive behind so obstinate an attention. How, I kept wondering, did a mind so vehement, so oriented toward itself, in perpetual fervor or frenzy, manage to be attracted by demonstrations so meticulous, so scandalously impersonal? It was only later, brooding over his explorations of drugs, that I understood what excesses of objectivity and rigor Michaux could achieve. His scruples were to lead him to a fetishism of the infinitesimal, of the imperceptible nuance, as much psychological as verbal, endlessly recapitulated with a breathless insistence. To reach vertigo by *investigation,* that seemed to me the secret of his enterprise. Read, in *L'Infini turbulent,* the page where he describes himself as "pierced by white," where everything is white, where "hesitation itself is white," and "horripilation" no less. After that there is no more white:

he has exhausted white, he has killed white. His obsession with the bottom of things makes him brutal: he liquidates appearance after appearance, not sparing one; he exterminates them by engulfing himself in them, by pursuing them precisely to their bottom — that bottom which is nonexistent, radically insignificant. . . . One English critic has found these soundings "terrifying." For me, on the contrary, they are positive and exalting in their impatience to disintegrate and to pulverize — by which I mean to discover and to know, truth in anything being merely the consummation of a sapping operation.

Though he classified himself among those who are "born tired," what has he ever done but flee delusion, excavate, search? Nothing, it is true, is so tiring as the effort toward lucidity, toward the vision without mercy. Apropos of a famous contemporary fascinated by that universal gangrene, History, he one day used a revealing expression: "spiritual blindness." Michaux himself, on the contrary, is someone who has abused the imperative to *see* within and around himself, to get to the bottom not only of an idea (which is easier than one thinks) but of the merest experience or impression: has he not subjected each of his sensations to a scrutiny that includes everything — torture, jubilation, will-to-conquest? This passion to apprehend himself, this exhaustive coming-to-consciousness, leads to an ultimatum he ceaselessly addresses, a devastating incursion into the darkest zones of his being.

It is from such a given that we must envision his revolt against his dreams, and the need he feels, despite the hegemony of psychoanalysis, to minimize them, to denounce them, to lay them open to ridicule. Disappointed by them, he delights in punishing them and in proclaiming their emptiness. But the real reason for his fury is perhaps less their nullity than their total independence of him, the privilege they enjoy of escaping his censorship, of hiding, of mocking and humiliating him by their mediocrity. Mediocre, yes, but autonomous, sovereign. It is in the name of consciousness, of becoming conscious as an exigence and a duty, and also out of wounded pride, that Michaux inculpates and calumnies them, that he lodges an indictment against them, a veritable challenge to the enthusiasms of the period. By discrediting the performances of the unconscious, he rids himself of the most precious illusion in circulation for over half a century.

All interior violence is contagious; his more than any other. One never leaves his presence demoralized. And it is of little consequence after all whether one frequents him assiduously or only on occasion, from the moment when, in all essential circumstances, one tries to imagine his reaction or his remarks: solitary, omnipresent, he is always there . . . , forever inseparable from what counts in an existence. This long-distance intimacy is possible only with an obsessive who is capable of impartiality, an introvert who is open to everything and disposed to speak of everything (even of current affairs). His views on the international situation, his diagnoses of political matters, are remarkably just and often prophetic. To have so exact a perception of the external world and at the same time manage to apprehend delirium *from within,* to traverse its many forms, to appropriate them, so to speak — one can accept this anomaly, so captivating, so enviable, as just that, without seeking to understand it. Yet I am going to suggest a necessarily approximate explanation. Nothing is more agreeable, at least for me, than a conversation with

Michaux about sickness. It is as if he had anticipated and feared all diseases, expected and fled them. . . . Any one of his books is a procession of symptoms, of threats glimpsed and in part made actual, infirmities pondered again and again. His sensibility to the diverse modalities of disequilibrium is prodigious. But politics, that sub-Promethean temptation, what is politics but a permanent and exasperated disequilibrium, the curse par excellence of a megalomaniac monkey? The least neutral mind, the least passive I know, could not help but be interested in politics, if only to wield his sagacity or his disgust. Writers in general, when they comment upon current events, display a laughable naïveté. It is important, it seems to me, to cite an exception. I believe I caught Michaux only once in flagrante delicto, not of naïveté (he is psychologically unfit for it) but of "good feelings," of confidence, of abandon, of something I translated at the time into terms it may be useful to give here:

"I admired him for his aggressive clear-sightedness, for his denials and his phobias, for the sum of his aversions. Last night, in the little street where we had been talking for hours, he told me, with quite an unexpected touch of emotion, that the idea of man's ultimate disappearance moved him. . . . Whereupon I left him, convinced I should never forgive him for that commiseration and that weakness."

If I extract this unspeakably naive note from an undated diary, it is to show that at the time what I especially prized in him was his incisive, tense, "inhuman" aspect, his explosions and his sneers, his flaying humor, his vocation as a convulsionary and a gentleman. Indeed, it seemed secondary that he was a poet. One day he confessed, I remember, that he sometimes wondered whether he was one. That he is a poet is obvious, but it is conceivable that *he might not have been one.*

What he is, much more obviously, I understood when I realized that as a young man, contemplating entering the priesthood, he devoured the mystics. I assert as fact that had he not been one himself, he would never have launched himself so methodically, so desperately, in pursuit of extreme states. Extreme, *this side of the absolute.* His works on drugs proceeded from the dialogue with the mystic he originally was, a repressed and sabotaged mystic waiting to take his revenge. If we were to collect all the passages in which Michaux deals with ecstasy, and if we were to suppress all references in them to mescaline or any other hallucinogen, would we not have the impression of reading explicitly religious experiences, inspired and not provoked, and deserving to figure in a breviary of unique moments and dazzling heresies? The mystics aspire not to subside into God but to exceed Him, swept on as they are by something remote, by a delirium of the ultimate, which we encounter among all those who have been visited and submerged by trance states. Michaux joins the mystics through his "inner gusts," his longing to attack the inconceivable, to force it, to break it open, to go beyond, without ever stopping, without retreating before any danger. Having neither the luck nor the misfortune to weigh anchor in the absolute, he creates his own abysses, provoking ever new ones, plunges into them and describes them. These abysses, it may be objected, are only *states.* No doubt. But for us everything is a state, and nothing but a state, consigned as we are to psychology ever since we were forbidden to wander in the Supreme. . . .

A true mystic, yet an unrealized one. We understand

Michaux insofar as he has undertaken everything in order not to conclude, keeping his irony at the very extremities to which his researches have led him. When he has reached some limit-experience, an "impure absolute" where he vacillates, where he no longer knows where he has come out, he never fails to resort to a familiar or comical turn of phrase, in order to make it clear that he is still himself, that he *remembers* that he is experimenting, that he will never completely identify himself with any of the moments of his quest. In all of these simultaneous excesses cohabit the ecstatic outbursts of an Angela di Foligno and the sarcasms of a Swift.

It is admirable that a man so constituted to destroy himself should have lived for many years in full possession of his vitality. "I take out the old man . . . , his damn body that breaks down, to which he clings so, our one body for the two of us," he writes in 1952, in *Vents et Poussières*. Always that interval between sensation and consciousness, always that superiority over what he is and over what he knows. . . . Thus he has managed, in his metaphysical perturbations — in his perturbations *tout court* — to remain, by the obsession of knowledge, external to himself. Whereas our contradictions and incompatibilities eventually subjugate and paralyze us, Michaux has succeeded in making himself the master of his, without slipping toward *sagesse*, without being swallowed up by it. All his life he has been tempted by India — merely tempted, fortunately, for if by some fatal metamorphosis he had ended by yielding to such enchantments, beclouded, he would have abdicated his prerogative of possessing more than one flaw that leads to wisdom and yet at the same time being fundamentally refractory to it.

What a catastrophe had he taken to Vedanta, or to Buddhism! He would have left his gifts there, his faculty for excess. Deliverance would have annihilated him as a writer: no more "gusts," no more torments, no more exploits. It is because he has not lowered himself to any formula of salvation, to any simulacrum of illumination, that frequenting him is so stimulating. He offers one nothing, he is what he is, he has no recipe for serenity, he continues, he feels his way, as if he were beginning. And he accepts one, on condition that one offers him nothing, either. Once again, a non-sage, a non-sage on his own. It astonishes me that he has not succumbed to so much intensity. It is true that his intensity is not of that accidental, fluctuating kind which is manifested in fits and starts: constant, flawless, it resides in itself and relies upon itself, it is inexhaustible precariousness, "intensity of being," an expression I borrow from the language of the theologians, the only one suitable to designate a success.

1973

14

Benjamin Fondane
6 Rue Rollin

✳

THE MOST CREASED and furrowed face one could imagine, a face with millennial wrinkles never still, animated as they were by the most contagious and the most explosive torment: I could not contemplate that countenance enough. Never before had I seen such harmony between appearance and utterance, between physiognomy and speech. Impossible for me to think of Fondane's slightest remark without immediately perceiving the imperious presence of his features.

I used to see him often (I knew him during the Occupation), always planning to stay no more than an hour, and I would end up spending the afternoon — it was my fault, of course, but his as well: he loved to talk, and I lacked the courage and still more the desire to interrupt a monologue that left me exhausted and enthralled. Yet it was I who was the garrulous one during my first visit, which I had paid with the intention of asking him some questions about Shestov. Probably out of a need to show off, I asked none at all, preferring to set forth the reasons

for my own interest in the Russian philosopher of whom
Fondane was the disciple — though less faithful than inspired. It may be apposite to note here that between the
two wars Shestov was very well known in Rumania, and
that his books were read more fervently there than elsewhere. Fondane had no idea of this and was greatly surprised to learn that in the country of his birth, we had
followed the same trajectory as he. . . . Wasn't there
something disturbing about this, and much more than a
coincidence? Many readers of Fondane's *Baudelaire* have
been struck by the chapter on boredom. I myself have always linked his predilection for this theme to his Moldavian origins. A paradise of neurasthenia, Moldavia is a
province of an unendurable dreary charm; in 1936 I spent
two weeks in Jassy, the capital, where if it had not been
for alcohol I would have foundered in the most dissolving
of depressions. Fondane loved to quote lines by Bacovia,
the laureate of Moldavian ennui, a boredom less refined
but much more corrosive than Baudelaire's "spleen." It is
an enigma to me that so many people manage not to die
of it. The experience of the "abyss" has, as we see, remote
sources.

Like Shestov, Fondane liked to start with a quotation,
a simple pretext to which he kept referring and from
which he drew unexpected conclusions. In his developments there was always, despite their subtlety, something
alluring; subtle he certainly was, he even abused his subtlety, it was his patent vice. In general, he couldn't stop —
he had the genius of *variation* — and it seemed, when one
listened to him, that he had a horror of the *period*. This
was glaringly apparent in his improvisations, as it was in
his books, especially *Baudelaire*. On several occasions he

told me he ought to cut a good many pages, and it is incomprehensible that he did not do so when we realize that he was living in the quasi-certainty of an imminent disaster. He believed himself to be threatened, and indeed he was, but it may be that inwardly he was resigned to the victim's lot, for without that mysterious complicity with the Ineluctable, and without a certain fascination with tragedy, there is no explanation for his rejection of all precautions, the most elementary of which was that of changing residences. (He was betrayed by his concierge!) A strange "unconcern" on the part of someone who was anything but naive, and whose psychological and political judgments testified to an exceptional perspicacity. I still have a very exact memory of one of my first visits, during which, after enumerating Hitler's dizzying faults and flaws, he launched into a visionary description of Germany's collapse, and this in such detail that I was convinced then and there that I was witnessing a delirium. It was only an anticipation of the facts.

In literary matters, I did not always share his tastes. He insistently recommended Hugo's book on Shakespeare, a virtually unreadable work that reminds me of a phrase recently used by an American critic to describe the style of *Tristes Tropiques:* "the aristocracy of bombast." The expression is a striking one, though unfair in that instance.

I understood better his partiality for Nietzsche, in whom he loved the foreshortenings that were so much denser than those of Novalis, about whom he had reservations. In truth he was always less interested in what an author said than in what he might have said, in what he *concealed;* in this he adopted Shestov's method — that is, the *peregrination through souls* much more than through doctrines. Uniquely sensitive to extreme cases, to the beguiling twists and turns in certain sensibilities, he once told me about a White Russian who had suffered in silence for eighteen years because he thought his wife was cheating on him. After so many years of mute torment, one day, unable to bear it any longer, he had it out with her, whereupon, after acquiring the certitude that all his suspicions had been false, incapable of enduring the notion that he had tortured himself for nothing over such a long period, he went into the next room and blew his brains out.

On another occasion, when he was describing his years in Bucharest, Fondane gave me an abject article attacking him, written by Tudor Arghezi, a great poet but a still greater pamphleteer, in prison at the time for political reasons (this was just after the First World War). Fondane, then a very young man, had managed to visit him there for some sort of interview. In return, the poet had proceeded to write a caricatural portrait so unspeakable that I have never been able to understand how Fondane could have shown it to me. He had his moments of detachment. . . . Usually indulgent, he ceased to be so toward those who supposed they had *found* . . . — those, in short, who converted to anything at all. He greatly esteemed Boris de Schloezer and was terrible disappointed to learn that the magisterial translator of Shestov could have *shifted* to Catholicism. He couldn't get over it and identified the occasion with a betrayal. *To search* was for him more than a necessity or an obsession — to search without stopping was a fatality, his fatality, perceptible even in his way of speaking, especially when he was enthusiastic or would vacillate continually between irony and breathlessness. I will forever blame myself for not having written down his remarks, his *trouvailles,* the leaps of a mind turning in all directions, constantly in combat with tyranny and the nullity of facts, greedy for contradictions and somehow in dread of *succeeding.*

I see him now, rolling cigarette after cigarette. Nothing, he used to say over and over again, equaled the pleasure of lighting up on an empty stomach. He kept on doing so despite a gastric ulcer that he proposed to deal with later, in a future about which he nursed no illusions. . . . The wife of his oldest friend told me at the time that she could not love him because of what she called his "sickly look." On his face he did not, it is true, bear the signs of prosperity, but everything in him was beyond sickness and health, as if both were merely stages he had transcended. Whereby he resembled an ascetic, an ascetic of a prodigious vivacity and verve that made one forget, while he was talking, his fragility, his vulnerability. But when he stopped talking — he who in spite of everything had mastered his fate — he gave the impression of dragging around something pitiful and, at certain moments, *lost.* The British poet David Gascoyne (who was also to suffer, under other circumstances, a tragic fate) told me that he had been haunted for months by the image of Fondane after he encountered him by chance on the Boulevard Saint-Michel on the day of Shestov's death. It will readily be understood why, even after thirty-three years, a being so fascinating is singularly present in my mind, and why, too, I never pass by Number 6 Rue Rollin without a pang.

1978

15

Borges

*

Letter to Fernando Savater

Paris, December 10, 1976

Dear Friend,

In November, during your visit to Paris, you asked me
to collaborate on a volume of tributes to Borges. My first
reaction was negative; my second . . . as well. What is
the use of celebrating him when the universities themselves
are doing so? The misfortune of being *recognized* has befallen him. He deserved better. He deserved to remain in
obscurity, in the Imperceptible, to remain as ineffable and
unpopular as nuance itself. There he was at home. Con-
secration is the worst of punishments — for a writer in
general, and particularly for a writer of his kind. Once
everyone starts quoting him, you must leave off; if you do
not, you feel you are merely swelling the ranks of his "admirers," of his enemies. Those who want to do him justice
at all costs are merely hastening his downfall. I shall stop
here, for if I continue in this style I shall end by pitying
his fate. And there is every reason to suppose he can do
that on his own.

I think I have already told you that if I was so interested in him, it was because he represented a vanishing specimen of humanity: he embodies the paradox of a sedentary man without an intellectual *patrie,* a stay-at-home adventurer at ease in several civilizations and literatures, a splendid and doomed monster. In Europe, as a kindred example, we may cite that friend of Rilke's, Rudolf Kassner, who early in this century published a work of the very first order about English poetry (it was after reading that book during the last war that I began to learn English . . .) and who spoke with admirable acuity of Sterne, of Gogol, of Kierkegaard, as well as of the Maghreb or of India. Normally depth and erudition do not go together, but he somehow reconciled them: a universal mind, lacking only grace, only seduction. It is here that Borges's superiority appears: incomparably seductive, he has managed to put a touch of the impalpable, the aerial, a wisp of *lace,* on everything, even on the most arduous reasoning. For in Borges everything is transfigured by the spirit of *play,* by a dance of dazzling *trouvailles* and delicious sophistries.

I have never been attracted by minds confined to a single form of culture. "Not to take root, not to belong to any community": such has been and such is my motto. Oriented toward other horizons, I have always wanted to know what was happening elsewhere; by the time I was twenty, the Balkan skyline had nothing more to offer me. This is the drama, and also the advantage, of being born in a minor "cultural" space. *The foreign* had become my god — whence that thirst to travel through literatures and philosophies, to devour them with a morbid ardor. What is happening in Eastern Europe must inevitably happen in the countries of Latin America, and I have noticed that its representatives are infinitely better informed, more "cultivated," than the incurably provincial Westerners. Neither in France nor in England do I see anyone who has a curiosity comparable to Borges's, a curiosity hypertrophied to the point of mania, to vice — I say "vice," for in matters of art and reflection, whatever does not turn into a somewhat perverse fervor is superficial, hence unreal.

As a student, I was led to investigate the disciples of Schopenhauer. Among them was a certain Philipp Mainlander, who particularly attracted me. Author of a *Philosophy of Deliverance,* he enjoyed the additional distinction, in my eyes, of having committed suicide. This completely forgotten philosopher, I flattered myself, belonged to me alone — not that there was any particular merit in my preoccupation: my studies had inevitably brought me to him. But imagine my astonishment when, much later, I came across a text by Borges that plucked him, precisely, out of oblivion! If I cite this example, it is because from that moment I began thinking more seriously than before about the condition of Borges, fated — *reduced* — to universality, constrained to exercise his mind in all directions, if only to escape the Argentine asphyxia. It is the South American void that makes the writers of an entire continent more open, more alive, and more diverse than those of Western Europe, paralyzed by their traditions and incapable of shaking off their prestigious sclerosis.

Since you ask what I like most about Borges, I have no hesitation in answering that it is his freedom in the most varied realms, his faculty of speaking with an equal subtlety of the Eternal Return and the Tango. For him *everything is equally worthwhile,* from the moment he is the center of everything. Universal curiosity is a sign of vitality only if it bears the absolute mark of a self, a self from which everything emanates and where everything ends up:

sovereignty of the arbitrary, beginning and end that can be interpreted according to the most capricious criteria. Where is reality in all this? The Self — that supreme farce. . . . Borges's playfulness reminds me of a certain romantic irony, the metaphysical exploration of illusion, juggling with the Infinite. Friedrich Schlegel, today, has his back to Patagonia. . . .

Once again, one can only deplore that an encyclopedic smile and a vision so refined should provoke general approbation, with all that implies. . . . But after all, Borges might become the symbol of a humanity without dogmas or systems, and if there is a utopia to which I should gladly subscribe, it would be the one where we all model ourselves on him — on one of the least ponderous minds that ever was, the last to give its true meaning to the word *select*.

16

Maria Zambrano
A Decisive Presence

✳

As SOON as a woman takes up philosophy, she becomes vain and aggressive, with all the reactions of a par-
venu. Arrogant yet uncertain, visibly *dumbfounded,* she is
not, evidently, in her element. How does it happen that
the uneasiness inspired by such a case is never felt in the
presence of Maria Zambrano? I have often asked myself
the question, and I believe I can answer it: Maria Zambrano has not sold her soul to the Idea, she has safe-
guarded her unique essence by setting the experience of
the Insoluble *above* reflection upon it, in short she has
transcended philosophy. . . . In her eyes, only what precedes or follows the formulated is true, only the word
wrested from the shackles of expression, or, as she herself
says magnificently, *La palabra liberada del lenguaje.*

She is one of those beings whom one regrets meeting
only too rarely but of whom one cannot stop thinking and
whom one longs to understand or at least to surmise. An
inner fire that eludes, an ardor that conceals itself beneath
an ironic resignation: everything in Maria Zambrano
leads to something else, everything involves an *elsewhere,*

everything. Though one can discuss anything at all with her, one is nonetheless sure to slide sooner or later toward crucial interrogations without necessarily following the meanders of reasoning. Hence a style of conversation unblemished by objectivity, a dialogue in which she leads one toward oneself, toward one's ill-defined pursuits, one's virtual perplexities. I remember precisely the moment when, at the Café de Flore, I made the decision to explore Utopia. On this subject, which we had mentioned in passing, she quoted a remark of Ortega's that she quite casually developed; I determined then and there to commit myself to the regret or the longing for the golden age — which I did not fail to do subsequently with a frenetic curiosity that little by little was to wear itself out or, rather, turn into exasperation. Nonetheless, readings extending over two or three years had their origin in that conversation.

Who, so much as she, has the gift, in anticipating one's anxiety, one's search, of dropping the unforeseeable and decisive word, the pregnant answer? And that is the reason one would like to consult her at life's turning points — on the threshold of a conversion, of a breakup, of a betrayal, at the moment of ultimate confidences, the heavy and compromising kind — so that she might offer one, somehow, a speculative absolution, and reconcile one as much to one's impurities as to one's impasses, one's stupors.

17

Weininger

*

Letter to Jacques Le Rider

Paris, December 16, 1982

Reading your book about my old and distant idol, I could not help remembering what an event *Geschlecht und Charakter* had been for me. This was in 1928; I was seventeen, and hungering for every form of excess and heresy, I delighted in deriving the ultimate consequences from an idea, extending rigor to aberration, to provocation, conferring upon frenzy the dignity of a system. In other words, I was passionate about everything, with the exception of nuance. In Weininger it was the dizzying exaggeration that fascinated me, the infinity of negation, the denial of common sense, the murderous intransigence, the search for an absolute position, the craving to carry a piece of reasoning to the point where it destroyed itself and ruined the structure to which it belonged. Add to this the obsession with the criminal and the epileptic (particularly in *Über die letzten Dinge*), the cult of the inspired formula and the arbitrary excommunication, the identifi-

cation of woman with Nothing and even with something
less. . . . To this devastating affirmation my adherence
was complete from the start. The object of my letter is to
acquaint you with the circumstance that incited me to espouse these extreme theses on the aforesaid Nothing. A
banal circumstance if ever there was one, yet it dictated
my conduct for several years. I was still in the Lycée, mad
about philosophy and about a girl in the Lycée as well.
One important detail: I did not know her personally,
though she belonged to the same milieu as I (the bourgeoisie of Sibiu, in Transylvania). As often happens with
adolescents, I was both insolent and timid, but my timidity
prevailed over my insolence. For over a year this torment
lasted, culminating one day when I happened to be reading some book or other, leaning against a tree in the town
park. Suddenly I heard giggling. Turning around, I saw —
who? *Her*, accompanied by one of the boys in my class,
the one scorned by us all and nicknamed The Louse. After
more than fifty years, I remember perfectly how I felt at
that moment. I forgo the details. The fact remains that I
vowed on the spot to abjure "sentiments." And that was
how I became a frequenter of brothels. A year after this
radical and commonplace disappointment, I discovered
Weininger. And found myself in the ideal situation to understand him. His splendid enormities concerning women
intoxicated me. How could I have been beguiled by a
subbeing? I kept asking myself. Why this torment, this calvary, on account of a fiction, a zero incarnate? A fated
figure had come at last to deliver me. But that deliverance
was to cast me into a superstition that he himself condemned, for I was drifting toward that "*Romantik der
Prostitution*" incomprehensible to serious minds and a
specialty of eastern and southeastern Europe. In any case,

my student life was passed under the spell of the Whore, in the shadow of her protective, cordial, even maternal, abasement. Weininger, by supplying me with the philosophical reasons for detesting an "honest" woman, cured me of "love" during the proudest and most frenetic period I have experienced in my life. I did not foresee a time when his indictments and his verdicts would no longer count for me except insofar as they would occasionally make me regret the *madman* I had been.

18

Fitzgerald
The Pascalian Experience
of an American Novelist

✳

FOR SOME, lucidity is a primordial gift, a privilege, even a sort of grace. They have no need to acquire it, to strain toward it; they are predestined to it. All their experiences concur to make them transparent to themselves. Stricken with clear-sightedness, they do not even suffer from it, so closely does it define them. If they live in a perpetual crisis, they accept that crisis quite naturally: it is immanent to their existence. For others, lucidity is a belated result, the fruit of an accident, of an internal rupture occurring at a specific moment. Hitherto, enclosed within an agreeable opacity, they adhered to the obvious aspects of things, without weighing or even divining their vacuity. Suddenly they are disabused and somehow engaged in spite of themselves in the career of knowledge; suddenly they are stumbling among unbreathable truths, for which nothing has prepared them. Hence they resent their new condition, regarding it not at all as a favor but as a "blow." Nothing prepared Scott Fitzgerald to face or to endure such unbreathable truths; the effort he made to adapt himself to them, however, has a pathos all its own.

"Of course all life is a process of breaking down, but the blows that do the dramatic side of the work — the big sudden blows that come, or seem to come, from outside — the ones you remember and blame things on and, in moments of weakness, tell your friends about, don't show their effect all at once. There is another sort of blow that comes from within — that you don't feel until it's too late to do anything about it, until you realize with finality that in some regard you will never be as good a man again."

These are not considerations by a brilliant, fashionable novelist. . . . *This Side of Paradise, The Great Gatsby, Tender Is the Night, The Last Tycoon:* if Fitzgerald had limited himself to those novels, he would present no more than a literary interest. Fortunately he is also the author of that text *The Crack-Up,* from which I have just quoted the opening and in which he describes his failure, his only great *success.*

As a young man, he was dominated by a single obsession: to become a "successful literary man." He did so. He experienced notoriety and even a genuine sort of glory. (An incomprehensible thing for me: T. S. Eliot wrote to Fitzgerald that he had read *The Great Gatsby* three times!) Money obsessed him: he wanted to make money, and he talked about it shamelessly. In his letters, as in his notebooks, he keeps coming back to it, to such a degree that we sometimes wonder whether we are in the presence of a writer or a businessman. Not that I dislike correspondence in which material problems are discussed; I prefer it a thousand times to the (falsely spiritualized) kind that slides over them or swathes them in poetry. But there is the manner and the tone. How many of Rilke's letters I once loved so much now seem insipid and bloodless! They never allude to the shabby side of penury. Intended for posterity, their "nobility" sickens me. The angels always live next door to the poor. Doesn't it seem that there's a certain offhandedness or a calculated naïveté in writing such things *at such length* in letters addressed to duchesses? To play the pure spirit borders on indecency. I don't believe in Rilke's angels; I believe even less in his poor. Too "distinguished," they lack cynicism, that salt of poverty. On the other hand, the letters of a Baudelaire or a Dostoyevsky, begging letters, touch me by their suppliant, desperate, gasping tone. You feel that they talk about money because they can't make any, that they were born poor and will remain poor, whatever happens. Poverty is consubstantial with them. They hardly aspire to success, since they know they can never achieve it. Now, what embarrasses me in Fitzgerald, in the early Fitzgerald, is that he aspires to success and achieves it. But fortunately, his success will be only a detour, an eclipse of his consciousness, before awakening to himself, to the revelation that he "will never be as good a man again." Fitzgerald died in 1940, at the age of forty-four; his crisis occurred around 1935–1936, the period when he wrote the articles that constitute *The Crack-Up*. Before this date, the crucial event in his life remained his marriage to Zelda. Together they led the artificial existence of Americans on the Côte d'Azur. Later he would describe his stay in Europe as "seven years of waste and tragedy," seven years when they indulged every extravagance, as though haunted by a secret desire to exhaust themselves, to empty themselves out. The inevitable happened: Zelda collapsed into schizophrenia and survived her husband only to die in an asylum fire. He had said of her, "Zelda is a case, and not a person." No doubt he meant that she was of interest only to psychiatry. He, on the other hand, would be a person: a case answerable to psychology or to history.

"My own happiness in the past often approached such an ecstasy that I could not share it even with the person dearest to me but had to walk it away in quiet streets and lanes with only fragments of it to distil into little lines in books — and I think that my happiness, or talent for self-delusion or what you will, was an exception. It was not the natural thing but the unnatural — unnatural as the Boom; and my recent experience parallels the wave of despair that swept the nation when the Boom was over."

I leave aside Fitzgerald's complacency in regarding himself as the expression of a "lost generation" or in interpreting his own crisis from external givens. For that crisis, if it emanated solely from a contingency, would lose all its scope. Insofar as they are specifically American, the revelations of *The Crack-Up* concern only literary history, or history itself. As inner experiences, however, they partake of an essence, of an intensity, that transcends contingencies and continents.

"What has just happened to me . . .": what had happened to Fitzgerald? He had lived in the intoxication of success, wanted happiness at all costs, aspired to become a writer of the first importance. Literally and figuratively, he had lived asleep. But then sleep left him. He began to wake, and what he discovered in his waking filled him with horror. A clear-sighted sterility submerged and paralyzed him.

Insomnia sheds a light on us which we do not desire but to which, unconsciously, we tend. We demand it in spite of ourselves, against ourselves. From it, and at the expense of our health, we seek something else: dangerous, harmful truths, everything that sleep has kept us from glimpsing. Yet our insomnia liberates us from our facility and our fictions only to confront us with a blocked horizon: *it illuminates our impasses*. It dooms us while it delivers us: an ambiguity inseparable from the experience of the night. This experience Fitzgerald tried in vain to escape. It assailed him, crushed him, it was too profound for his spirit. Would he turn to God? He detested lying — which is to say that he had no access to religion. The nocturnal universe rose before him like an absolute. Nor had he any access to metaphysics, though he would be forced toward it. Obviously he was not ripe for his nights.

"The horror has come now like a storm — what if this night prefigured the night after death — what if all thereafter was an eternal quivering on the edge of an abyss, with everything base and vicious in oneself urging one forward and the baseness and viciousness of the world just ahead. No choice, no road, no hope — only the endless repetition of the sordid and the semi-tragic. Or to stand forever, perhaps, on the threshold of life unable to pass it and return to it. I am a ghost now as the clock strikes four."

In truth, aside from the mystic and the man who is prey to a grand passion, who is really ripe for his nights? We may desire to lose sleep if we are believers, but if we are without any certainty, how to remain for hours and hours in a tête-à-tête with ourselves? We can reproach Fitzgerald for not divining the importance of the night as an occasion for or a method of knowledge, as an enriching disaster, but we cannot remain insensitive to the pathos of his vigils, when the "repetition of the sordid and the semi-tragic" was for him the consequence of his denial of God, of his incapacity to be an accomplice in the greatest metaphysical fraud, in the supreme lie of our nights.

"Now the standard cure for one who is sunk is to consider those in actual destitution or physical suffering — this is an all-weather beatitude for gloom in general and fairly salutory day-time advice for everyone. But at three o'clock in the morning, a forgotten package has the same tragic importance as a death sentence, and the cure doesn't work — and in a real dark night of the soul it is always three o'clock in the morning, day after day."

The daytime truths have no validity in the "real dark night of the soul." And instead of blessing it as a source of revelations, Fitzgerald curses that night, identifies it with his collapse, and denies it all value as knowledge. *He has a Pascalian experience without the Pascalian spirit.* Like all frivolous men, he trembles at venturing further into himself. Yet a fatality impels him onward. He resists extending his being to its limits, and he reaches them in spite of himself. The extremity to which he accedes, far from being the result of a plenitude, is the expression of a broken spirit: it is the boundlessness of the Flaw, it is the negative experience of the infinite. His sickness plunges down to the very sources of affectivity. This he will explain himself in a text that gives us the key to his troubles:

"I only wanted absolute quiet to think out why I had developed a sad attitude toward sadness, a melancholy attitude toward melancholy and a tragic attitude toward tragedy — *why I had become identified with the objects of my horror or compassion.*"

A crucial text, a sick man's text. In order to understand its importance, let us try to define, by contrast, the behavior of the healthy man, the active man. Let us grant ourselves, to this effect, a supplement of health. . . .

However contradictory and intense our states, normally we master them, we manage to neutralize them:

"health" is the faculty we possess of keeping a certain distance from them. A well-balanced being always manages to slide over his depths or to thread his way across his own abysses. Health — the condition of action — presupposes a flight from oneself, a desertion of ourselves. No true action without the fascination of the *object*. When we act, our inner states count only by their relation to the external world; they have no intrinsic value, hence it is permissible for us to master them. If we should happen to be sad, we are so *on account* of a specific situation, an incident, or a distinct reality.

The sick man proceeds entirely otherwise. He realizes his states in themselves — his sadness sadly, his melancholy melancholically — and he espouses, he experiences, all tragedy tragically. He is merely *subject*, and nothing but. If he identifies himself with the objects of his horror or of his compassion, these objects constitute for him only various modalities of himself. To be sick is to coincide totally with oneself.

"Every act of life from the morning tooth-brush to the friend at dinner had become an effort . . . I saw that even my love for those closest to me was become only an attempt to love, that my casual relations were only what I remembered I *should* do, from other days."

Divorce from reality, which Zelda was to know in its irreparable aspect, Fitzgerald was lucky enough to experience in an attenuated form: a schizophrenia for litterateurs. . . . Let us add — another piece of luck for him — that he was expert at "self-pity." His abuse of it preserved him from total ruin. This is not a paradox. An excess of sympathy for ourselves preserves our reason, for such brooding over our miseries proceeds from an alarm in our vitality, from a reaction of energy, at the same time that it expresses an elegiac disguise of our instinct of self-preservation. Have no pity for those who pity themselves; they will never give way altogether. . . .

Fitzgerald survived his crisis without surmounting it completely. He hoped nonetheless to find a balance between "the sense of the futility of effort and the sense of the necessity to struggle; between the conviction of the inevitability of failure and still the determination to succeed." His being, he thought, would then continue its course "as an arrow shot from nothingness to nothingness with such force that only gravity would bring it to earth at last."

These fits of pride were accidental. Deep in himself, he would have liked to return, in his relations with men, to the subterfuges of conventional existence; he would have liked to *retreat*. To do so, he would assume a mask.

"A smile — ah, I would get me a smile. I'm still working on that smile. It is to combine the best qualities of a hotel manager, an experienced old social weasel, a headmaster on visitors' day, a colored elevator man, . . . a trained nurse coming on a new job, a body-vendor in her first rotogravure, a hopeful extra swept near the camera. . . ."

His crises would lead him not to mysticism or to a final despair or to suicide, but to disillusion. "The sign CAVE CANEM is hung permanently just above my door. I will try to be a correct animal though, and if you throw me a bone with enough meat on it I may even lick your hand." He was enough of an aesthete to modify his misanthropy with irony and to introduce a note of elegance into the economy of his disasters. His casual style lets us glimpse what we might call the charm of a broken life. I should even add that one is "modern" to the degree that one is sensitive to this charm. Reaction of the disabused, no doubt — of individuals who, incapable of resorting to a metaphysical background or to a transcendent form of salvation, cling to their woes with complacency, as to accepted defeats. Disillusion is the equilibrium of the defeated. And it was as a defeated man that Fitzgerald, after conceiving the pitiless truths of *The Crack-Up,* went to Hollywood to look for success — always success — in which, moreover, he could no longer believe. At the end of a Pascalian experience, to write screenplays! In his last years, it was as if he no longer aspired to anything but compromising his abysses, swallowing his neuroses — as if, in his heart of hearts, he felt himself unworthy of the downfall he had just suffered. "I speak with the authority of failure," he had said one day. Except that with time, he degraded this failure, stripped it of all its spiritual value. Nor should we be surprised: in the "real dark night of the soul," he struggled more as a victim than as a hero. The same is true of all those who live their drama solely in terms of psychology; unsuited to perceiving an exterior absolute to combat or to yield to, they eternally relapse into themselves in order to vegetate, ultimately, *beneath* the truths they have glimpsed. They are, once again, disillusioned, for disillusion — retreat after a defeat — is characteristic of the individual who cannot destroy himself by a disaster, nor endure it to the end in order to triumph over it. Disillusion is the "semi-tragic" hypostatized. And since Fitzgerald could not remain worthy of his own drama, we cannot count him among those of high anguish. The interest he offers for us consists precisely in that disproportion between the inadequacy of his means and the extent of anxiety that he experienced.

A Kierkegaard, a Dostoyevsky, a Nietzsche override

their own experiences, like their "spells," because they are *worth* more than what "happens" to them. Their destiny precedes their life. This is not so for Fitzgerald: his existence is inferior to what it discovers. The culminating moment of his life he saw only as a disaster for which he could not console himself, despite the revelations he gained from it. *The Crack-Up* is a novelist's "season in hell" — by which we have no intention of minimizing the scope of a testimony in itself overwhelming. A novelist who wants to be nothing but a novelist undergoes a crisis that for a certain time projects him outside the lies of literature. He wakens to certain truths that devastate his awareness, the repose of his spirit — a rare event in the world of letters where sleep is de rigueur, an event that in the case that concerns us has not always been grasped in its true signification. Thus Fitzgerald's admirers deplore the fact that he brooded over his failure and, by dint of ruminating so deeply upon it, spoiled his literary career. We, on the contrary, deplore that he did not remain sufficiently loyal to that failure, that he did not sufficiently explore or exploit it. It is a second-order mind that cannot chose between literature and the "real dark night of the soul."

1955

19

Guido Ceronetti
The Body's Hell

✳

Letter to the Editor

Paris, March 17, 1983

You have asked me, dear friend, what sort of man is the author of *Le Silence du corps*. Your curiosity is understandable, for one cannot read this book without constantly wondering about the admirable monster who conceived it. I must admit that I have actually met him only during his visits to Paris, but I am frequently in contact with him by telephone and by letter. And also, in an indirect fashion, through a person as astonishing as he, an Italian girl of nineteen whom he partly brought up and who, two years ago, came to Paris for a stay of some months. Of an amazing intellectual maturity for her age, she frequently reacted like a very young girl, even like a child, and this mélange of inspired acuity and ingenuousness made it impossible to forget her for a single instant. She penetrated your life; she was truly a presence, an enchanted creature visited by sudden terrors that increased both her woes and her charms. She was even more present in Guido's thoughts and cares. I cannot, of course, go into details, though there is nothing suspect or improper to conceal. As if it were yesterday I can see the two of them in the Luxembourg on a rainy November afternoon: he pale, grim, oppressed, leaning forward, and she, disturbing, unreal, taking her tiny swift steps after him. As soon as I caught sight of them, I hid behind a tree. The day before, I had received a letter from him — the most heartrending anyone had ever sent me. Their sudden appearance in the empty park left me with an impression of distress, of desolation, that has pursued me for a long time. I have forgotten to tell you that at our first meeting, his expression of being nowhere, of fundamental unbelonging, of predestination to exile here on earth, made me think immediately of Prince Myshkin. (Moreover, the letter in question had a Dostoyevskian accent throughout.) For her, he was unassailable; he alone escaped the devastating judgments that she passed on everyone else. She unreservedly adopted his vegetarian fanaticism. Not to eat as other people do is more serious than not to think as they do; Guido's alimentary principles — no, his dogmas — are of a rigor that makes the manuals of ascesis read like invitations to gluttony and debauch. I myself am quite obsessive about my diet, but compared to the two of them I seem no better than a cannibal. If you do not feed yourself as others do, you do not take care of yourself as others do, either. Impossible to imagine Guido going into a pharmacy. One day he called me from Rome to ask me to buy him, in a health-food store run by a young Vietnamese, a certain Japanese yam, apparently very effective against arthritis. According to Guido, all you have to do is rub it on your joints, and the pain will stop immediately. All the acquisitions of the modern world are hateful to him; everything revolts him, even health, if it is due to chemistry. And yet his book, which incontestably emanates from a demand for purity, attests to an undeniable craving for horror, as if he were an eremite seduced by hell. By the hell of the body. A sure sign of failing and, indeed, of threatened health: to feel one's organs, to be *conscious* of them, to the point of obsession. The curse of dragging about a corpse is the very theme of this book. From beginning to end, a procession of physiological secrets that fill you with dread. You have to admire the author's courage in reading so many ancient and modern treatises of gynecology — certainly a terrifying task, one likely to discourage for good even the most hardened satyr. A voyeur's heroism in the matter of suppurations, a curiosity excited by the supreme anti-poetry of menstruation, by hemorrhages of all kinds, and by the most intimate miasmas, by the fetid universe of pleasure, the "tragedy of the physiological functions." "The parts of the body that smell the strongest are those that contain the most soul"; "All the soul's excretions, all the mind's diseases, all the blackness of life, and that's what we call *love.*"

Reading *Le Silence du corps,* I was reminded several times of Huysmans, particularly of his biography of Saint Lydwine of Schiedam. Except in the essentials, sanctity is answerable to the aberrations of the organs, to a series of anomalies, to an inexhaustible variety of disorders, and this is true of whatever is profound, intense, unique. No interior excesses without an inadmissible substratum; the most ethereal ecstasy recalls in certain aspects the most crass. Is Guido a connoisseur of derangements disguised as a man of erudition? Sometimes I think so, but ultimately not. For if he has an evident weakness for corruption, on the other hand he is equally solicited by what is purest in the visionary or despairing wisdom of the Old Testament. Has he not — admirably — translated Job, Ecclesiastes, and Isaiah? Here we are no longer in pestilence and horror, but in lamentation and outcry. Here is someone who lives, according to a profound necessity and sometimes according to his moods, on different spiritual levels. His last book (*La Vie apparente*) illustrates these contradictory temptations, preoccupations that are both immediate and timeless. What one most loves in him is the avowal of his defeats: "I am a failed ascetic," he confides, rather embarrassed. A providential failure, for on its account we are sure of understanding each other, of really belonging to the *perduta gente*. Had he taken the decisive step toward salvation (how easy it is to conceive of him as a monk!), we should have been deprived of a delicious companion, filled with imperfections, manias, and moods, one whose elegiac inflections match his vision of a world so obviously doomed. Just listen to him: "How can a pregnant woman read a newspaper without immediately aborting?" "How can we judge abnormal and mentally diseased those who are terrified by the human face?"

If you were to ask me what ordeals he passed through, I would not be in a position to answer. All I can tell you is that the impression he gives is of someone *wounded* — like all those, I am tempted to add, to whom the gift of illusion has been denied.

Do not be afraid of meeting him: of all creatures, the least intolerable are those who hate human beings. Never run away from a misanthrope.

20

She Was Not of Their World . . .

✳

I ONLY MET HER TWICE. Seldom enough. But the extraordinary is not to be measured in terms of time. I was instantly conquered by her air of absence and bewilderment, her whisperings (she didn't *speak*), her uncertain gestures, her glances that did not adhere to people or things, her quality of being an adorable specter. . . . "Who are you? Where do you come from?" were the questions you wanted to ask her right away. She wouldn't have been able to answer, so identified was she with her mystery, so reluctant to betray it. No one will ever know how she managed to breathe — by what aberration she yielded to the claims of breath — nor what she was seeking among us. The one sure thing is that she was not from here, and that if she shared our fallen state it was merely out of politeness or some morbid curiosity. Only angels and incurables inspire a sentiment analogous to the one you felt in her presence. Fascination, supernatural malaise!

The first moment I saw her, I fell in love with her timidity, a unique, unforgettable timidity that gave her the appearance of a vestal exhausted in the service of a secret god, or else of a mystic ravaged by the nostalgia or the abuse of ecstasy, forever unfit to reinstate the surfaces of life!

Overwhelmed by possessions, fortunate according to the world, she nonetheless seemed utterly destitute, on the threshold of an ideal beggary, doomed to murmur her poverty at the heart of the Imperceptible. Moreover, what could she own and utter, when silence stood for her soul and perplexity for the universe? And did she not suggest those creatures of lunar light that Rozanov speaks of? The more you thought about her, the less you were inclined to regard her according to the tastes and views of time. An unreal kind of malediction weighed upon her. Fortunately, her charm itself was inscribed within the past. She should have been born elsewhere, and in another age, in the mist and desolation of the moors around Haworth, beside the Brontë sisters. . . .

Knowing anything about faces, you could readily see in hers that she was not doomed to endure, that she would be spared the nightmare of the years. Alive, she seemed so little the accomplice of life that you could not look at her without thinking you would never see her again. *Adieu* was the sign and the law of her nature, the flash of her predestination, the mark of her passage on earth; hence she bore it like a nimbus, not by indiscretion, but by solidarity with the invisible.

21

Foreshortened Confession

✳

I WANT TO WRITE only in an explosive state, in a fever or under great nervous tension, in an atmosphere of settling accounts, where invectives replace blows and slaps. It usually begins this way: a faint trembling that becomes stronger and stronger, as after an insult one has swallowed without responding. Expression means a belated reply, or else postponed aggression: I write in order not to take action, to avoid a crisis. Expression is relief, the indirect revenge of one who cannot endure shame and who rebels *in words* against his kind, against himself. Indignation is not so much a moral as a literary impulse; it is, indeed, the wellspring of inspiration. And wisdom? Just the opposite. The sage in us ruins all our best impulses; he is the saboteur who diminishes and paralyzes us, who lies in wait for the madman within in order to calm and compromise him, in order to dishonor him. Inspiration? A sudden disequilibrium, an inordinate pleasure in affirming or destroying oneself. I have not written a single line at my normal temperature. And yet for years on end I regarded myself as the one individual exempt from flaws.

Such pride did me good: it allowed me to blacken paper. I virtually ceased *producing* when my delirium abated and I became the victim of a pernicious modesty, deadly to that ferment from which intuitions and truths derive. I can produce only if, the sense of absurdity having suddenly abandoned me, I esteem myself the beginning and the end. . . .

Writing is a provocation, a fortunately false view of reality that sets us *above* what is and what seems to be. . . . To rival God, even to exceed Him by the mere virtue of language: such is the feat of the writer, an ambiguous specimen, torn and infatuated, who, having forsaken his natural condition, has given himself up to a splendid vertigo, always dismaying, sometimes odious. Nothing more wretched than the word, yet it is by the word that one mounts to sensations of felicity, to an ultimate dilation where one is completely alone, without the slightest feeling of oppression. The Supreme achieved by syllables, by the very symbol of fragility! It can also be achieved, oddly, by irony, on the condition that the latter, carrying its demolition work to extremes, dispenses shudders of a god in reverse. Words as agents of an ecstasy inside out. . . . Everything that is truly intense partakes of paradise and hell, with this difference, that the former we can only glimpse, whereas we have the luck to perceive and, better still, to *feel* the latter. There exists an even more notable advantage, on which the writer has a monopoly — that of ridding himself of his *dangers*. Without the faculty of blackening pages, I wonder what I would have become. To write is to get free of one's remorse and one's rancors, to vomit up one's secrets. The writer is an unbalanced being who uses those words to cure himself. How many disorders, how many grim attacks have I not trimphed over thanks to these insubstantial remedies!

Writing is a vice one can weary of. In truth, I write less and less, and I shall doubtless end up no longer writing at all, no longer finding the least charm in this combat with others and with myself.

When one attacks a subject, however ordinary, one experiences a feeling of plenitude, accompanied by a touch of arrogance. A phenomenon stranger still: that sensation of superiority when one describes a figure one admires. In the middle of a sentence, how easily one believes oneself the center of the world! Writing and worship do not go together: like it or not, to speak of God is to regard Him *from on high*. Writing is the creature's revenge, and his answer to a botched Creation.

22

Rereading . . .

＊

Translated into German by Paul Celan, my *Précis de Décomposition* (*A Short History of Decay*) was published by Rowohlt in 1953. When it was republished in Germany in 1978, the editor of *Akzente* asked me to introduce it to the magazine's readers. That is the origin of this text.

REREADING THIS BOOK, which is now over thirty years old, I try to recognize the person I was — a person who escapes me to some degree. My gods were Shakespeare and Shelley. I still frequent the former; the latter, rarely. I cite him to indicate the kind of poetry that intoxicated me. An untidy lyricism matched my dispositions; unfortunately, I discern traces of it in all my efforts of the period. Who can still read a poem like *Epipsychidion*? I used to read it, in any case, with delight. Shelley's hysterical Platonism repels me now, and to effusion, whatever its form, I prefer concision, rigor, a deliberate coldness. My vision of things has not fundamentally changed; what certainly has changed is the *tone*. The content of thought is rarely modified in any real way; what does undergo a metamorphosis, on the other hand, is the turn of phrase, appearance, rhythm. Growing old, I have noticed that poetry is less and less necessary to me: perhaps one's taste for it is linked to a surplus of vitality? I have an increasing tendency — *fatigue* must have a lot to do with it — toward dryness, toward laconism, at the expense of explosion. Now, the *Précis* was an explosion. Writing it, I had the impression I was escaping a sense of oppression, with which I could not have continued for long: I had to breathe, I had to *break out.* I felt the need to come to decisive terms, not so much with men as with existence as such, which I would have liked to provoke to single combat, if only to see *which of us* would win. I had, to be frank, a quasi-certitude that I would gain the upper hand, that it would be impossible for existence to triumph. To corner existence, to force it into its last hiding places, to reduce it to nothingness by frenzied reasonings and accents recalling Macbeth or Kirilov: such was my ambition, my intention, my dream, the program of my every moment. One of the first chapters is called "The Anti-Prophet." As a matter of fact, I reacted as a prophet, assigned myself a mission — a corrosive one, if you like, but a mission all the same. By attacking the prophets, I was attacking myself and . . . God, according to my principle in those days, which was that one should be concerned solely with Him and with oneself. Whence the uniformly violent tone of an ultimatum (not succinct, as it should have been, but verbose, diffuse, insistent), of a challenge addressed to Heaven and earth, to God and to God's *ersatz* — in short, to *everything.* In the desperate fury of those pages, where it would be bootless to look for a grain of modesty, of serene and resigned reflection, of acceptance and respite, of smiling fatalism, it is the unbridled madness of my youth as well as an incoercible love of denial that attain their apogee. What has always beguiled me in negation is the power of substituting oneself for everyone and everything, of being a sort of demiurge, of *possessing* the world, as if one had collaborated in its advent and then had the right, even the duty, to precipitate its ruin. Destruction, immediate consequence of the spirit of negation, corresponds to a profound instinct, to a type of jealousy that each of us must experience in his heart of hearts with regard to the First Being, to His position and the idea He represents and symbolizes. However much I have frequented the mystics, deep down I have always sided with the Devil; unable to equal him in power, I have tried to be worthy of him, at least, in insolence, acrimony, arbitrariness, and caprice.

After the Spanish publication of the *Précis,* two Andalusian students asked me if it was possible to live without *"fundamentación."* I answered that it was true that I had found no solid basis anywhere and that I had nonetheless managed to endure, for with the years one got used to everything, even vertigo. Then, too, one does not constantly keep watch and interrogate oneself, absolute lucidity being incompatible with breathing. If one were at every moment conscious of what one knew — if, for example, the sentiment of foundationlessness were both continual and intense — one would kill oneself or allow oneself to slip into imbecility. One exists thanks to the moments when one *forgets* certain truths; this is because during such intervals one accumulates energy, and it is energy that permits one to confront those selfsame truths. When I despise myself, I tell myself, in order to shore up my confidence, that after all, I have managed to maintain myself in being or in a semblance of being, with a perception of things that very few could have endured. Several young people in France have told me that the chapter that most attracted them was "The Automaton," that intolerable quintessence. In my way I must be a fighter, since I have not succumbed to my ruminations.

The two students also asked me why I had not stopped writing and publishing. Not everyone has the luck to die young, was my answer. My first book, with its sonorous title — *On the Summits of Despair* — I wrote in Rumanian at the age of twenty-one, while promising myself never to begin another. Then I committed a second, with the same promise subsequently. The farce has been repeated for over forty years. Why? Because writing, however little, has helped me pass from one year to the next, the *expressed* obsessions being weakened and — halfway — overcome. To produce is an extraordinary comfort. And to publish, another. To have a book coming out, that is your life, or a part of your life that becomes external to you, that no longer belongs to you, that has ceased to torment you. Expression diminishes you, impoverishes you, lifts weights off you: expression is loss of substance, and liberation. It drains you, hence it saves you, it strips you of an encumbering overflow. When you detest someone to the point of wanting to liquidate him, the best thing is to take a sheet of paper and to write on it any number of times that X is a bastard, a fool, a monster, and you will immediately discover that you hate him less and that you are no longer thinking quite so much about vengeance. This is more or less what I did with regard to myself and the world. The *Précis* I drew from my lower depths in order to insult life and insult myself. The result? I have endured myself a little better, as I have better endured life. You look after yourself as best you can.

*   *   *

The first version of the book was written very quickly in 1947 and was called "Negative Exercises." I showed it to a friend, who gave it back to me a few days later, saying "You have to rewrite the whole thing." I deeply resented his advice, but luckily I took it. In fact, I rewrote the thing three times, for on no account did I want it to be considered as the work of a foreigner. My ambition was nothing less than to compete with the natives. Where could such effrontery have come from? My parents, who spoke only Rumanian and Hungarian and a little German, knew no French words except *bonjour* and *merci*. This was the case with almost everyone in Transylvania. When I went to Bucharest in 1929 for some sort of studies, I realized that most intellectuals there spoke French fluently; this produced in me, who read French and no more, a fury that would last for a long time and that still endures, in another form: since reaching Paris, I have never been able to rid myself of my Wallachian accent. If I cannot speak like the natives, at least I shall try to write like them: this must have been my unconscious reasoning; otherwise, how explain my desperate eagerness to do as well as they and even — insane presumption — better than they?

The efforts we expend to assert ourselves, to measure ourselves against our kind and, if possible, to outstrip them, have vile, inadmissible, hence powerful, reasons. The noble resolutions, on the contrary, issuing from a desire for effacement, inevitably lack vigor, and we quickly abandon them, with or without regret. Everything by which we excel proceeds from a murky and suspect source — from our depths, in fact.

And there is also this: I should have chosen any other language than French, for I have little in common with its distinguished vaunt; it is at the antipodes of my nature, of my outbursts, of my true self and my kind of wretchedness. In its rigidity, in the quantity of elegant constraints that it represents, French seems to me an exercise in ascesis or, rather, the combination of a straitjacket and a salon. Yet it is precisely on account of this incompatibility that I have attached myself to this language, to the point of exulting when the great New York scholar Erwin Chargaff (born, like Paul Celan, in Czernowitz) confided to me one day that for him *only what was expressed in French deserved to exist. . . .*

Today, when this language is in full decline, what saddens me most is to perceive that the French themselves do not seem to mind. And it is I, a Balkan reject, who suffer at seeing it go under. Well then, I shall sink, inconsolable, with it!